THE PROBLEM SOLVER'S TOOLKIT

CREATIVE SOLUTIONS FOR BUSINESS CHALLENGES

DR. MINAKSHI BANSAL

DEDICATION

*To all the trailblazers, the innovators, the dreamers,
and the doers who dare to challenge the status quo
and seek creative solutions to the world's problems.
Your courage and perseverance inspire us all.*

❦❦❦

Contents

About The Author   *ix*

Preface   *xiii*

1. Reframing The Challenge: Shifting Perspectives For Innovative Solutions.   1

Part 1

2. Brainstorming Beyond Boundaries: Unleashing The Power Of Collective Creativity.   7

Part 2

3. Root Cause Analysis: Digging Deep To Unearth The Underlying Issue.   13

Part 3

4. Design Thinking: Empathizing With Users To Create Impactful Solutions.   19

Part 4

5. Lean Methodology: Eliminating Waste And Optimizing Processes.   25

Part 5

6. SWOT Analysis: Assessing Strengths, Weaknesses, Opportunities, And Threats.   31

Part 6

7. Scenario Planning: Preparing For Potential Futures And Mitigating Risks.   37

Part 7

8. Decision Matrix: Evaluating Options Objectively And Choosing The Best Path.   43

Part 8

Contents

9. Mind Mapping: Visualizing Connections And Unlocking New   49

Ideas.

Part 9

10. Storytelling: Harnessing The Power Of Narrative To Engage   55

And Inspire.

Part 10

11. Gamification: Transforming Work Into Play To Boost   61

Motivation And Engagement.

Part 11

12. Collaboration: Leveraging Collective Intelligence For Better   67

Results.

Part 12

13. Experimentation: Embracing Failure As A Learning   73

Opportunity.

Part 13

14. Prototyping: Building Quick, Iterative Models To Test And   79

Refine Ideas.

Part 14

15. Agile Development: Adapting To Change And Delivering   85

Value Incrementally.

Part 15

16. Data-Driven Decision Making: Using Insights To Inform And   91

Optimize Choices.

Part 16

17. Customer Journey Mapping: Understanding Customer Needs   97

And Pain Points.

Contents

Part 17

   18. Feedback Loops: Continuously Improving Through Feedback 103
   And Iteration.

Part 18

   19. Innovation Culture: Fostering An Environment That Embraces 109
   Change And Experimentation.

Part 19

   20. Diversity And Inclusion: Harnessing The Power Of Different 115
   Perspectives.

Part 20

   21. Change Management: Leading Teams Through Transitions 121
   Smoothly.

Part 21

   22. Continuous Learning: Staying Ahead Of The Curve With New 127
   Skills And Knowledge.

Part 22

   23. SUMMARY 133

Citation and References 137

Other Books of the Author 139

CONTACT 145

About The Author

This book represents the culmination of extensive research and meticulous analysis, incorporating a diverse range of sources, including numerous books, scholarly studies, and personal experiences. Additionally, I have scoured various websites to gather relevant information and data essential for the compilation of this work. I have taken every precaution to ensure the accuracy of the information presented and have diligently cited all sources to acknowledge their contributions.

From her earliest days, Minakshi was distinguished by an insatiable appetite for reading. Her literary universe was inhabited by characters and narratives that spanned ethical tales, motivational and inspirational stories, and the mythic parables imbued with life lessons. This voracious reading habit was not merely for personal edification but was driven by a desire to distill and disseminate the essence of these narratives to foster the development of students and peers alike. She was particularly captivated by the lives and teachings of historical figures and spiritual leaders such as Adi Shankaracharya, Swami Vivekananda, Dr. APJ Abdul Kalam, Mahamana Pandit Madan Mohan Malviya, Mahatma Gandhi, Sardar Vallabhai Patel, and Vinoba Bhave, among others. Their philosophies and life stories fueled her ambition to embody their ideals of resilience, selflessness, and relentless pursuit of knowledge.

Dr. Minakshi's academic and practical engagement with psychology has been equally noteworthy. As a research scholar, her focus has been on exploring the intricate tapestry of the human psyche, aiming to unlock the potential for psychological well-being and societal harmony. Her scholarly work is complemented by her active involvement in social work, where she employs her academic insights to make tangible differences in the lives of the underprivileged. Her endeavours in social work are characterized by an innovative approach that combines traditional wisdom with contemporary psychological practices to address the multifaceted challenges faced by these communities.

Her artistic talents, another facet of her diverse capabilities, are not merely a personal passion but also serve as a medium through which she communicates and connects with others. Her art, rich in symbolism and emotional depth, reflects her philosophical inquiries and social concerns, offering viewers a glimpse into the breadth of her intellect and the depth of her compassion.

In addition to her contributions to the arts and social sciences, Dr. Minakshi has embraced the healing arts of Pranic Healing, mastering the techniques developed by Master Choa Kok Sui. This practice, which focuses on the manipulation of Prana or life energy to heal the body and aura, has been both a personal journey of discovery and a means through which she extends her healing touch to others. Her proficiency in Pranic Healing is complemented by her advocacy and teaching of various forms of meditation aimed at rejuvenation, personal betterment, and the cultivation of harmony within individuals and communities alike.

Dr. Minakshi's life is a narrative of relentless pursuit, not just of personal achievement but of the upliftment and empowerment of society at large. Her diverse interests and talents—spanning the arts, literature, psychology, and the healing practices—converge on a singular path of service. She embodies the spirit of the luminaries who inspired her, channelling their legacy through her actions and teachings. Through her books, art, and social initiatives, she continues to inspire a new generation to embark on their own journeys of self-discovery, resilience, and altruism.

Her commitment to social betterment, particularly her focus on uplifting underprivileged children, reflects a deep understanding of the transformative potential of education and personal development. By integrating her knowledge of psychology, her artistic sensibilities, and her healing practices, Dr. Bansal has developed a holistic approach to social work that addresses both the immediate needs and the long-term well-being of the communities she serves.

As an author, Dr. Minakshi's writings offer a blend of inspirational insights, practical wisdom, and reflective contemplations drawn from her extensive reading and life experiences. Her books serve as a guide for those seeking to navigate the complexities of life with grace, resilience, and purpose. Through her narratives, she extends an invitation to her readers to explore the depths of their own potential and to contribute meaningfully to the collective well-being of society.

In Dr. Minakshi Bansal, we find a remarkable synthesis of the artist, the scholar, the healer, and the social activist. Her life's work stands as a beacon of hope and a source of inspiration for individuals seeking to make a difference in the world. Her story is a compelling reminder of the power of individual action, rooted in compassion and driven by a profound commitment to the betterment of humanity. Dr. Minakshi's legacy is not just in the tangible outcomes of her efforts but in the enduring spirit of inquiry, empathy, and service that she embodies.

ᎠᎠᎠ

Preface

In the ever-evolving landscape of business, challenges are an inevitable part of the journey. Whether you are a seasoned executive, a budding entrepreneur, or a team leader navigating the complexities of the modern workplace, the ability to effectively solve problems is a critical skill that can make or break your success. This book, born out of my years of experience as a consultant, strategist, and problem-solver, is a culmination of the lessons I've learned, the strategies I've developed, and the insights I've gained along the way.

It is my firm belief that problem-solving is not merely a skill but a mindset. It is a way of approaching challenges with curiosity, creativity, and resilience. It is about embracing the unknown, challenging assumptions, and finding innovative solutions that drive growth and create value. This book is designed to equip you with a toolkit of practical strategies and frameworks that can help you develop this problem-solving mindset and apply it to the challenges you face in your own professional journey.

Each chapter in this book delves into a specific aspect of problem-solving, providing you with a deep understanding of the concepts, tools, and techniques that can be leveraged to tackle a wide range of business challenges. From reframing problems and brainstorming beyond boundaries to leveraging data-driven insights and fostering a culture of innovation, this book covers a broad spectrum of topics that are essential for effective problem-solving.

The first few chapters focus on the foundational aspects of problem-solving. We begin by exploring the power of reframing, which involves shifting perspectives to unlock new possibilities and find creative solutions. We then delve into brainstorming, a time-tested technique for generating ideas and fostering collaboration. We also explore the importance of root cause analysis, a systematic approach to uncovering the underlying causes of problems and implementing effective solutions.

As we progress through the book, we delve into more advanced topics, such as Design Thinking, a human-centric approach to problem-solving that prioritizes empathy and user needs. We also explore Lean Methodology, a powerful framework for eliminating waste and optimizing processes. We then delve into the world of data-driven decision-making, where insights gleaned from data can inform and optimize choices.

The book also delves into the importance of soft skills in problem-solving. We explore the power of storytelling to engage and inspire, the benefits of collaboration and leveraging collective intelligence, and the importance of continuous learning to stay ahead of the curve. We also discuss the role of innovation culture in fostering an environment that embraces change and experimentation.

Throughout the book, I share real-world examples and case studies that illustrate how these tools and strategies have been successfully applied in various business contexts. These stories serve as inspiration and provide practical guidance on how to implement these concepts in your own organization.

In addition to the theoretical frameworks and practical tools, this book also emphasizes the importance of mindset and attitude in problem-solving. It encourages readers to embrace challenges as opportunities for growth, to view failure as a learning experience, and to cultivate a spirit of curiosity and experimentation. It also emphasizes the importance of collaboration, communication, and leadership in driving successful problem-solving efforts.

This book is not a magic bullet that will instantly solve all your problems. It is a guide, a roadmap, a toolkit that can empower you to tackle challenges with confidence and creativity. It is my hope that by reading this book, you will gain a deeper understanding of the problem-solving process, develop new skills and strategies, and ultimately, become a more effective problem solver in your personal and professional life.

The challenges facing businesses today are complex and multifaceted, requiring a holistic and adaptable approach to problem-solving. This book provides a comprehensive framework for navigating these challenges, drawing on a wide range of disciplines, from psychology and sociology to engineering and design. It is my hope that this book will serve as a valuable resource for anyone who seeks to become a more effective problem solver and make a positive impact in their organization and the world.

I invite you to embark on this journey of discovery and exploration with me. As you delve into the pages of this book, I encourage you to reflect on your own experiences, challenge your assumptions, and experiment with new approaches. Remember, the most effective problem solvers are those who are willing to learn, adapt, and evolve. So, embrace the challenges, embrace the unknown, and embrace the power of problem-solving. The future is yours to create.

Dr. Minakshi Bansal
Social Activist
Ahmedabad, Gujarat, Bharat

ᘐᘐᘐ

ONE

REFRAMING THE CHALLENGE: SHIFTING PERSPECTIVES FOR INNOVATIVE SOLUTIONS.

In the complex and ever-evolving landscape of modern business, challenges are an inevitable part of the journey. Whether it's a sudden market disruption, a decline in sales, or an internal operational issue, every obstacle presents an opportunity for growth and innovation. However, the path to overcoming these challenges often lies not in brute force or conventional thinking, but in the subtle art of reframing.

Reframing is the process of intentionally shifting one's perspective on a problem or situation. It involves moving beyond the initial assumptions and limitations to explore alternative viewpoints, uncover hidden opportunities, and unlock creative solutions. This shift in perspective can be a game-changer, transforming seemingly insurmountable obstacles into stepping stones for progress.

One of the fundamental principles of reframing is the recognition that our perception of a problem is not the problem itself. Our minds are wired to create mental models, simplifying complex realities into manageable concepts. While these models can be useful for navigating everyday life, they can also limit our ability to see the bigger picture and identify novel solutions. By consciously challenging our assumptions and questioning the validity of our mental models, we open ourselves up to new possibilities.

A classic example of reframing in action is the story of Kodak, the once-dominant photography company. For decades, Kodak's success was built on its expertise in film-based photography. However, with the advent of digital photography, the company found itself struggling to adapt. Kodak's initial response was to defend its existing business model, focusing on improving film technology and resisting the digital revolution. This defensive approach ultimately proved to be a fatal mistake.

Had Kodak reframed the challenge, it might have recognized that the rise of digital photography was not simply a threat, but also an opportunity. Instead of viewing digital cameras as a competitor to film, Kodak could have embraced the new technology and leveraged its existing strengths in imaging and optics to become a leader in the digital space. By failing to reframe, Kodak missed out on a chance to reinvent itself and ultimately fell victim to its own success.

The process of reframing can be broken down into several key steps. The first step is to identify the existing frame. This involves articulating the problem as it is currently understood, including the underlying assumptions, constraints, and goals. This step is crucial because it forces us to confront the limitations of our current thinking and opens up space for new perspectives.

Once the existing frame has been identified, the next step is to challenge its validity. This can be done by asking questions such as: "What are we assuming to be true?" "Are these assumptions accurate?" "What other ways could we look at this problem?" "What are the potential consequences of our current approach?" By questioning the existing frame, we create a sense of cognitive dissonance that motivates us to seek alternative viewpoints.

The third step is to generate new frames. This can be done through a variety of techniques, such as brainstorming, mind mapping, and role-playing. The goal is to come up with as many different perspectives on the problem as possible, no matter how outlandish or impractical they may seem. The more frames we generate, the greater the chance of finding a truly innovative solution.

Once a new frame has been identified, the final step is to evaluate its potential. This involves considering the feasibility, desirability, and viability of the solution that emerges from the new frame. Does the solution address the root cause of the problem? Is it aligned with the organization's values and goals? Can it be implemented effectively? If the answer to these questions is yes, then the new frame has the potential to unlock a breakthrough solution.

Reframing is not always easy. It requires a willingness to let go of familiar patterns of thought and embrace uncertainty. It also demands a certain level of creativity and open-mindedness. However, the rewards of reframing can be immense. By shifting our perspectives, we can unlock new insights, identify hidden opportunities, and develop innovative solutions that were previously unimaginable.

In the context of business challenges, reframing can be applied to a wide range of issues. For example, a company facing declining sales might reframe the problem as an opportunity to improve customer service or develop new products. A team struggling with internal conflict might reframe the situation as a chance to strengthen communication and collaboration. By reframing the challenge, we can transform a negative situation into a positive catalyst for change.

The benefits of reframing extend beyond the immediate problem at hand. By cultivating a habit of reframing, we can develop a more flexible and adaptable mindset, enabling us to navigate the complexities of the modern world with greater ease. We can also foster a culture of innovation within our organizations, encouraging employees to challenge the status quo and explore new possibilities.

In conclusion, reframing is a powerful tool for problem-solving and innovation. By consciously shifting our perspectives, we can unlock hidden opportunities, generate creative solutions, and overcome seemingly insurmountable challenges. Whether it's a personal dilemma or a business crisis, reframing offers a path to growth and transformation. By embracing the power of reframing, we can unleash our full potential and achieve extraordinary results.

ᑭᑭᑭ

Reframing is the art of turning obstacles into opportunities. By shifting perspectives, we unlock new possibilities and discover innovative solutions that were previously hidden. Remember, the way we see the problem is not the problem itself.

TWO

Brainstorming Beyond Boundaries: Unleashing the Power of Collective Creativity.

In the quest for innovative solutions and groundbreaking ideas, businesses often turn to brainstorming as a tried-and-true method. However, traditional brainstorming sessions can sometimes fall short, stifled by limitations and conventional thinking. To truly unleash the power of collective creativity, it is essential to go beyond boundaries and embrace a more expansive approach to brainstorming.

At its core, brainstorming is a group creativity technique designed to generate a large number of ideas for solving a problem or achieving a goal. It typically involves a group of people coming together to share their thoughts and suggestions in a free-flowing and non-judgmental environment. While this basic format can be effective in some cases, it often fails to tap into the full potential of the group's collective intelligence.

To move beyond the limitations of traditional brainstorming, it is important to understand the underlying principles that drive creativity. Creativity is not simply about coming up with new ideas; it is about making connections between seemingly disparate concepts, challenging assumptions, and exploring uncharted territory. It is a process of discovery and experimentation, fueled by curiosity and a willingness to take risks.

One of the key factors that can hinder creativity in brainstorming sessions is the fear of judgment. When people feel that their ideas will be evaluated or criticized, they are less likely to share their most original and unconventional thoughts. To overcome this barrier, it is essential to create a safe and supportive environment where everyone feels comfortable expressing their ideas, no matter how outlandish they may seem.

Another factor that can limit creativity is the tendency to get stuck in familiar patterns of thinking. When we approach a problem with preconceived notions and assumptions, we are less likely to see alternative solutions. To break free from these mental constraints, it is important to encourage divergent thinking, which involves generating a wide range of ideas without evaluating their feasibility or practicality.

One way to foster divergent thinking is to use prompts or stimuli that are unrelated to the problem at hand. For example, instead of asking participants to brainstorm ideas for a new marketing campaign, you could ask them to describe their favorite childhood toy or to imagine what the world would be like if gravity didn't exist. These seemingly unrelated prompts can spark new connections and insights that can then be applied to the problem at hand.

Another technique for promoting divergent thinking is to encourage participants to build on each other's ideas. This can be done through a process called "brainwriting," in which participants write down their ideas on individual slips of paper and then pass them around to other members of the group. Each person then adds their own thoughts and suggestions to the original idea, creating a chain of interconnected concepts.

In addition to divergent thinking, it is also important to encourage convergent thinking, which involves evaluating and refining the ideas that have been generated. This can be done through a process of discussion and debate, in which participants weigh the pros and cons of different ideas and try to reach a consensus on the best solution.

One effective method for facilitating convergent thinking is to use a decision matrix, which is a tool for evaluating options based on a set of criteria. The criteria can be anything from feasibility and cost to potential impact and alignment with organizational goals. By systematically evaluating each idea against the criteria, the group can narrow down the options and identify the most promising solutions.

To truly unleash the power of collective creativity, it is essential to go beyond the traditional brainstorming format and embrace a more holistic approach that incorporates a variety of techniques and strategies. This might involve combining brainstorming with other creativity tools, such as mind mapping, storytelling, or role-playing. It might also involve incorporating elements of play and experimentation, such as using games or simulations to explore different scenarios.

Ultimately, the key to successful brainstorming is to create an environment that is conducive to creativity and innovation. This means fostering a culture of openness, trust, and respect, where everyone feels valued and empowered to contribute their unique perspectives. It also means providing the necessary resources and support to enable participants to explore their ideas and turn them into reality.

By going beyond boundaries and embracing a more expansive approach to brainstorming, businesses can tap into the full potential of their collective creativity and generate truly innovative solutions to their most pressing challenges. Whether it's a new product, a marketing campaign, or a business strategy, the power of collective creativity can unlock a world of possibilities.

Brainstorming is not just about generating ideas; it's about harnessing the power of collective creativity. When we come together and share our diverse perspectives, we can spark new insights and develop solutions that surpass individual efforts. Don't be afraid to think outside the box and embrace the unexpected.

THREE

ROOT CAUSE ANALYSIS: DIGGING DEEP TO UNEARTH THE UNDERLYING ISSUE.

In the intricate web of business operations, problems are an inevitable reality. These problems can manifest in various forms, from declining sales and customer complaints to production delays and employee dissatisfaction. While addressing the immediate symptoms of these problems may offer temporary relief, it is crucial to delve deeper and unearth the underlying root causes to achieve lasting solutions. This is where the invaluable tool of Root Cause Analysis (RCA) comes into play.

RCA is a systematic approach to problem-solving that aims to identify the fundamental reasons behind a problem's occurrence. Unlike superficial fixes that merely treat the symptoms, RCA seeks to understand the underlying causes that contribute to the problem's existence. By addressing these root causes, organizations can prevent the problem from recurring and implement effective, long-term solutions.

At its core, RCA is based on the principle that problems are often interconnected and multi-faceted. A single problem may have multiple root causes, and each of these causes may be linked to other underlying issues. Therefore, RCA requires a comprehensive and methodical approach that considers all potential factors that may contribute to the problem.

The first step in conducting RCA is to clearly define the problem. This involves gathering data, analyzing trends, and interviewing stakeholders to gain a thorough understanding of the problem's scope and impact. A well-defined problem statement serves as a guide for the entire RCA process, ensuring that the investigation remains focused and relevant.

Once the problem is clearly defined, the next step is to identify potential root causes. This can be done through various methods, such as brainstorming, fishbone diagrams, and the 5 Whys technique. Brainstorming involves generating a list of possible causes through open discussion and collaboration. Fishbone diagrams, also known as Ishikawa diagrams, help visualize the relationship between the problem and its potential causes by categorizing them into different branches. The 5 Whys technique involves repeatedly asking "why" to delve deeper into each potential cause until the root cause is identified.

As potential root causes are identified, it is essential to gather evidence to support or refute their validity. This can be done through data analysis, experiments, and further investigation. It is important to remain objective and unbiased during this process, avoiding the temptation to jump to conclusions or rely on assumptions.

Once the root causes have been identified and validated, the next step is to develop and implement corrective actions. These actions should be designed to address the root causes directly, rather than simply treating the symptoms. They should also be feasible, sustainable, and aligned with the organization's goals and values.

Implementing corrective actions is not the end of the RCA process. It is crucial to monitor the effectiveness of these actions and make adjustments as needed. This can be done through regular reviews, feedback loops, and ongoing data analysis. By continuously monitoring and improving the implemented solutions, organizations can ensure that the problem is truly resolved and prevent it from recurring in the future.

RCA is a versatile tool that can be applied to a wide range of problems, from technical issues to human errors and organizational challenges. It can be used in various industries, including manufacturing, healthcare, service, and government. The benefits of RCA are numerous. By addressing the root causes of problems, organizations can:

Prevent recurrence: RCA helps organizations identify and eliminate the underlying causes of problems, preventing them from happening again in the future.

Improve efficiency: By addressing the root causes of inefficiencies, RCA can help organizations streamline their processes and improve productivity.

Enhance quality: RCA can help organizations identify and address the root causes of quality issues, leading to improved products and services.

Reduce costs: By preventing problems from recurring and

improving efficiency, RCA can help organizations reduce costs associated with rework, waste, and customer dissatisfaction.

Foster a culture of continuous improvement: RCA encourages a proactive approach to problem-solving, fostering a culture of continuous improvement within the organization.

While RCA is a powerful tool, it is not without its challenges. It can be a time-consuming process that requires a significant investment of resources. It also requires a willingness to challenge assumptions and embrace change. However, the benefits of RCA far outweigh the challenges, making it an essential tool for any organization that seeks to improve its performance and achieve long-term success.

In conclusion, Root Cause Analysis is a systematic and methodical approach to problem-solving that focuses on identifying and addressing the underlying causes of problems. By digging deep and uncovering the root causes, organizations can implement effective, long-term solutions that prevent problems from recurring and improve overall performance. RCA is a versatile tool that can be applied to a wide range of issues, from technical problems to human errors and organizational challenges. By embracing RCA, organizations can foster a culture of continuous improvement, enhance quality, reduce costs, and achieve lasting success.

The path to true resolution lies in understanding the root cause of a problem. By digging deep and uncovering the underlying issues, we can address the source rather than merely treating the symptoms. Root Cause Analysis is not just a tool, but a mindset of continuous improvement.

FOUR

DESIGN THINKING: EMPATHIZING WITH USERS TO CREATE IMPACTFUL SOLUTIONS.

In the ever-evolving landscape of business and innovation, the ability to create impactful solutions is paramount. Traditional problem-solving methods often fall short, focusing on technical aspects while neglecting the human element. Design Thinking, a human-centric approach, has emerged as a powerful methodology to address this gap. By prioritizing empathy and understanding user needs, Design Thinking enables organizations to develop solutions that resonate with their target audience, ultimately leading to greater success and satisfaction.

At its core, Design Thinking is a non-linear, iterative process that involves a deep understanding of users, challenging assumptions, redefining problems, and creating innovative solutions. It is a mindset that encourages collaboration, experimentation, and a willingness to embrace ambiguity. While often associated with product design, its principles can be applied to a wide range of challenges, from service design to organizational change.

The foundation of Design Thinking lies in empathy, the ability to understand and share the feelings of others. In the context of problem-solving, empathy involves stepping into the shoes of the user, experiencing the world from their perspective, and understanding their needs, motivations, and pain points. This deep level of understanding allows designers to identify unmet needs and uncover hidden opportunities for innovation.

To cultivate empathy, Design Thinking encourages immersive research techniques. Interviews, observations, and user testing are just a few of the methods used to gather insights into user behavior, preferences, and challenges. By actively listening to users and observing them in their natural environment, designers can gain a nuanced understanding of their needs and desires.

The next step in the Design Thinking process is to define the problem. This involves synthesizing the insights gathered during the empathy stage and framing the problem in a human-centric way. Rather than focusing on technical specifications or business goals, the problem statement should highlight the user's needs and aspirations. By clearly defining the problem from the user's perspective, designers set the stage for developing solutions that truly address their needs.

Once the problem is defined, the ideation stage begins. This is where creativity and divergent thinking come into play. Designers brainstorm a wide range of potential solutions, encouraged to think outside the box and explore unconventional ideas. The goal is not to find the perfect solution immediately, but to generate a diverse set of possibilities that can be further refined and developed.

Prototyping is a crucial step in the Design Thinking process. It involves creating tangible representations of potential solutions, whether they are physical mockups, digital prototypes, or role-playing scenarios. Prototypes allow designers to test their ideas in a low-risk environment, gather feedback from users, and iterate on their designs. This iterative process helps refine the solution and ensure that it meets the user's needs in a practical and effective way.

The final stage of Design Thinking is testing. This involves putting the prototype in the hands of users and observing how they interact with it. User feedback is invaluable at this stage, as it helps identify any flaws or shortcomings in the design. Designers can then use this feedback to further refine the solution and ensure that it is user-friendly and effective.

The benefits of Design Thinking extend far beyond product development. By prioritizing empathy and user needs, organizations can create solutions that are not only functional but also meaningful and impactful. This approach fosters a deeper connection between organizations and their customers, leading to increased loyalty, satisfaction, and advocacy.

In addition to improving customer experiences, Design Thinking can also drive innovation within organizations. By encouraging collaboration, experimentation, and a willingness to challenge assumptions, it can spark new ideas and uncover hidden opportunities for growth. Design Thinking can also be used to tackle complex social challenges, such as poverty, inequality, and climate change.

However, implementing Design Thinking is not without its challenges. It requires a shift in mindset, a willingness to embrace ambiguity, and a commitment to collaboration. Organizations may need to invest in training and resources to equip their teams with the necessary skills and tools. Additionally, Design Thinking can be a time-consuming process, requiring patience and perseverance.

Despite these challenges, the potential rewards of Design Thinking are significant. By putting users at the center of the design process, organizations can create solutions that truly meet their needs, drive innovation, and ultimately achieve greater success. Whether it's a new product, a service, or an organizational change, Design Thinking offers a powerful framework for creating impactful solutions.

In conclusion, Design Thinking is a human-centric approach to problem-solving that prioritizes empathy, collaboration, and experimentation. By understanding user needs and challenges, designers can develop solutions that are not only functional but also meaningful and impactful. While it requires a shift in mindset and a commitment to collaboration, the potential rewards of Design Thinking are significant. By embracing this approach, organizations can unlock their creative potential, drive innovation, and create a lasting impact on the world.

ᑭᑭᑭ

Empathy is the heart of Design Thinking. By stepping into the shoes of our users and understanding their needs, we can create solutions that truly resonate and make a meaningful impact. Remember, the best designs are those that prioritize the human experience.

FIVE

LEAN METHODOLOGY: ELIMINATING WASTE AND OPTIMIZING PROCESSES.

In the relentless pursuit of efficiency and value creation, businesses across industries have increasingly turned to Lean Methodology as a guiding principle. Born out of the Toyota Production System (TPS) in the mid-20th century, Lean Methodology has evolved into a comprehensive approach to eliminating waste and optimizing processes. By focusing on delivering value to customers while minimizing resource consumption, Lean Methodology has revolutionized the way organizations operate, leading to significant improvements in productivity, quality, and customer satisfaction.

At its core, Lean Methodology is a mindset that emphasizes continuous improvement and the relentless pursuit of perfection. It is a philosophy that permeates every aspect of an organization, from the shop floor to the executive suite. The fundamental premise of Lean is that any activity or process that does not add value to the customer is considered waste and should be eliminated or minimized. This includes activities such as overproduction, waiting, unnecessary transportation, excess inventory, defects, over-processing, and underutilized talent.

To identify and eliminate waste, Lean Methodology employs a variety of tools and techniques. Value Stream Mapping (VSM) is a visual representation of the entire process, from raw materials to finished products or services. By mapping out the flow of materials and information, organizations can identify bottlenecks, redundancies, and other sources of waste. Once the waste is identified, Lean tools such as 5S (Sort, Set in Order, Shine, Standardize, Sustain) and Kaizen (continuous improvement) can be used to eliminate it and streamline the process.

One of the key principles of Lean Methodology is the concept of "pull" production. In traditional "push" systems, products are manufactured or services are delivered based on forecasts and schedules, often leading to overproduction and excess inventory. In a "pull" system, production is triggered by customer demand, ensuring that only the necessary amount of products or services are produced, thus minimizing waste and reducing inventory costs.

Another important aspect of Lean Methodology is the focus on empowering employees. Lean encourages employees at all levels to identify and solve problems, continuously improve processes, and take ownership of their work. This is achieved through a variety of techniques, such as standardized work, visual management, and problem-solving tools like the A3 report. By empowering employees, Lean creates a culture of continuous improvement where everyone is invested in the success of the organization.

Lean Methodology has been successfully implemented in a wide range of industries, from manufacturing and healthcare to service and government. In manufacturing, Lean has led to significant reductions in lead times, inventory levels, and defects, while improving quality and customer satisfaction. In healthcare, Lean has been used to streamline patient flow, reduce waiting times, and improve the overall patient experience. In service industries, Lean has helped organizations improve customer service, reduce costs, and increase efficiency.

Despite its proven success, implementing Lean Methodology is not without its challenges. It requires a significant change in mindset and culture, as well as a commitment to continuous improvement. It also requires a willingness to invest in training and resources to support the implementation process. However, the benefits of Lean far outweigh the challenges, making it an essential tool for any organization that seeks to improve its performance and achieve long-term success.

One of the most significant benefits of Lean Methodology is its focus on customer value. By eliminating waste and optimizing processes, Lean enables organizations to deliver products and services that meet or exceed customer expectations while minimizing costs. This leads to increased customer satisfaction, loyalty, and repeat business.

Lean Methodology also promotes a culture of continuous improvement. By empowering employees to identify and solve problems, Lean fosters a sense of ownership and engagement. This leads to a more motivated and productive workforce, which in turn drives innovation and growth.

In addition to improving customer satisfaction and employee engagement, Lean Methodology can also have a positive impact on the bottom line. By eliminating waste and optimizing processes, Lean can lead to significant reductions in costs, improved quality, and increased efficiency. This can translate into higher profits, increased market share, and a stronger competitive position.

However, to realize the full benefits of Lean Methodology, organizations must be willing to embrace change and challenge the status quo. Lean is not a quick fix or a one-time project; it is a continuous journey of improvement. It requires a long-term commitment from leadership and a willingness to invest in training and resources.

In conclusion, Lean Methodology is a powerful approach to eliminating waste and optimizing processes. By focusing on delivering value to customers while minimizing resource consumption, Lean has revolutionized the way organizations operate. Through its emphasis on continuous improvement, employee empowerment, and customer focus, Lean has proven to be a valuable tool for improving productivity, quality, and customer satisfaction. While implementing Lean can be challenging, the benefits far outweigh the costs, making it an essential strategy for any organization that seeks to thrive in today's competitive business environment.

ppp

Waste is the enemy of efficiency. By adopting Lean Methodology and eliminating non-value-adding activities, we can streamline processes, reduce costs, and deliver greater value to our customers. Every step in a process should contribute to the final goal.

SIX

SWOT ANALYSIS: ASSESSING STRENGTHS, WEAKNESSES, OPPORTUNITIES, AND THREATS.

In the intricate dance of business strategy, a keen understanding of one's position in the market landscape is paramount. Enter SWOT analysis – a powerful framework that empowers organizations to dissect their internal strengths and weaknesses, while simultaneously scanning the external environment for opportunities and threats. This comprehensive assessment serves as a compass, guiding decision-makers towards informed choices that capitalize on strengths, mitigate weaknesses, seize opportunities, and counter threats.

At its core, SWOT analysis is a structured approach to evaluating a company's competitive position. By examining the four quadrants – Strengths, Weaknesses, Opportunities, and Threats – businesses gain a holistic view of their internal capabilities and the external forces that shape their industry. This analysis provides a foundation for crafting effective strategies, setting realistic goals, and making sound decisions.

Strengths, the first quadrant of the SWOT matrix, represent the internal attributes and resources that give a company a competitive edge. These can include a strong brand reputation, a loyal customer base, a talented workforce, proprietary technology, efficient operations, or a robust financial position. Identifying and leveraging these strengths is crucial for sustained success. For instance, a company with a strong brand reputation can leverage this asset to launch new products or enter new markets with greater ease.

Weaknesses, the second quadrant, are the internal limitations that hinder a company's performance. These can range from outdated technology and inefficient processes to a lack of skilled personnel or a weak financial position. Recognizing and addressing these weaknesses is essential for mitigating risks and improving overall competitiveness. For example, a company with outdated technology may need to invest in upgrading its systems to remain competitive.

Opportunities, the third quadrant, are external factors that a company can exploit to its advantage. These can include emerging markets, changing consumer preferences, new technologies, or regulatory shifts. Identifying and seizing these opportunities is crucial for growth and innovation. For instance, a company that recognizes a growing demand for eco-friendly products can capitalize on this trend by developing and marketing sustainable offerings.

Threats, the final quadrant, are external factors that pose risks to a company's performance. These can include economic downturns, increased competition, disruptive technologies, or unfavorable regulatory changes. Recognizing and mitigating these threats is essential for ensuring long-term survival and success. For example, a company facing increased competition may need to differentiate its products or services to maintain market share.

The power of SWOT analysis lies in its ability to integrate internal and external perspectives. By examining both the company's internal capabilities and the external environment, businesses can gain a comprehensive understanding of their competitive landscape. This holistic view allows them to identify strategic options, prioritize initiatives, and allocate resources effectively.

However, SWOT analysis is not without its limitations. It is a snapshot in time, capturing a company's position at a specific moment. The business landscape is constantly evolving, so SWOT analysis should be conducted regularly to ensure that the assessment remains relevant and accurate. Additionally, SWOT analysis can be subjective, with different individuals or teams interpreting the same information differently. To mitigate this, it is important to involve a diverse group of stakeholders in the analysis process, ensuring that a variety of perspectives are considered.

To conduct a SWOT analysis, businesses can follow a structured approach. The first step is to assemble a cross-functional team representing different departments and perspectives. This team should then brainstorm and identify the company's strengths, weaknesses, opportunities, and threats. It is important to be thorough and honest during this process, avoiding the temptation to gloss over weaknesses or overstate strengths.

Once the SWOT factors have been identified, the next step is to prioritize them. Not all factors are created equal, and some will have a greater impact on the company's performance than others.

This prioritization can be done using a variety of methods, such as ranking, weighting, or scoring.

With the prioritized SWOT factors in hand, the final step is to develop strategies. These strategies should aim to leverage strengths, mitigate weaknesses, seize opportunities, and counter threats. For example, a company with a strong brand reputation might develop a strategy to expand into new markets, while a company with outdated technology might invest in upgrading its systems.

SWOT analysis is not a one-size-fits-all tool. The specific strategies that emerge from the analysis will depend on the unique circumstances of each company. However, the process of conducting a SWOT analysis can provide valuable insights that inform strategic decision-making and drive long-term success.

In conclusion, SWOT analysis is a powerful framework for assessing a company's competitive position. By examining internal strengths and weaknesses, as well as external opportunities and threats, businesses can gain a comprehensive understanding of their market landscape. This understanding can then be used to develop effective strategies that leverage strengths, mitigate weaknesses, seize opportunities, and counter threats. While SWOT analysis has its limitations, it remains an invaluable tool for guiding strategic decision-making and driving long-term success.

ᐳᐳᐳ

In the game of business, knowing your strengths and weaknesses is crucial, but understanding the opportunities and threats in your environment is equally important. SWOT analysis is your compass, guiding you towards strategic decisions that capitalize on strengths, mitigate weaknesses, seize opportunities, and counter threats.

SEVEN

Scenario Planning: Preparing for potential futures and mitigating risks.

In the intricate tapestry of business, the future is a realm of both promise and uncertainty. Market dynamics shift, technologies evolve, and unforeseen events can disrupt even the most meticulously laid plans. To navigate this uncertain terrain, organizations have increasingly turned to scenario planning, a strategic foresight methodology that empowers them to anticipate potential futures, assess their implications, and develop robust strategies to mitigate risks and seize opportunities.

Scenario planning is not about predicting the future with absolute certainty. Rather, it is about exploring a range of plausible futures, considering both positive and negative outcomes, and preparing for a variety of eventualities. By envisioning multiple scenarios, organizations can better understand the potential impacts of different trends and events, identify potential risks and opportunities, and develop flexible strategies that can adapt to changing circumstances.

At its core, scenario planning is a structured process that involves several key steps. The first step is to identify the key drivers of change that are likely to shape the future of the industry or market in question. These drivers can be economic, technological, social, political, environmental, or a combination of these factors. By understanding the forces that are driving change, organizations can better anticipate the potential scenarios that may unfold.

Once the key drivers of change have been identified, the next step is to develop a set of plausible scenarios. These scenarios should be internally consistent, plausible, and relevant to the organization's strategic goals. They should also be diverse enough to capture a range of possible outcomes, including both optimistic and pessimistic scenarios. Each scenario should be described in detail, outlining the specific events, trends, and outcomes that define it.

The third step is to assess the implications of each scenario for the organization. This involves analyzing the potential impacts of each scenario on the organization's operations, financial performance, competitive position, and overall strategic goals. The goal is to understand how different scenarios would affect the organization and to identify potential risks and opportunities associated with each scenario.

The fourth step is to develop strategies for each scenario. These strategies should be designed to mitigate the risks and seize the opportunities associated with each scenario. They should also be flexible enough to adapt to changing circumstances. For example, a company might develop a strategy to expand into new markets if a scenario of economic growth unfolds, while also preparing a contingency plan to cut costs if a scenario of economic downturn materializes.

The final step is to monitor the environment for signs of change and adjust strategies as needed. Scenario planning is not a one-time exercise; it is an ongoing process that requires constant vigilance and adaptation. By regularly reviewing and updating their scenarios, organizations can ensure that their strategies remain relevant and effective in the face of evolving circumstances.

Scenario planning offers several key benefits for organizations. First, it helps organizations to think more broadly and creatively about the future. By considering a range of possible outcomes, organizations can break free from linear thinking and develop more innovative and adaptable strategies. Second, scenario planning helps organizations to identify and mitigate risks. By anticipating potential threats and developing contingency plans, organizations can reduce their vulnerability to unforeseen events and improve their resilience. Third, scenario planning helps organizations to seize opportunities. By identifying potential opportunities and developing strategies to capitalize on them, organizations can accelerate their growth and achieve their strategic goals.

Scenario planning is not without its challenges. It can be a time-consuming and resource-intensive process, requiring significant investment in research, analysis, and collaboration. Additionally, scenario planning requires a willingness to confront uncertainty and embrace ambiguity. However, the benefits of scenario planning far outweigh the challenges, making it an essential tool for any organization that seeks to thrive in today's complex and rapidly changing business environment.

In conclusion, scenario planning is a powerful methodology for preparing for potential futures and mitigating risks. By exploring a range of plausible scenarios, assessing their implications, and developing flexible strategies, organizations can navigate uncertainty with greater confidence and resilience. Scenario planning is not a crystal ball, but it is a valuable tool for anticipating change, identifying risks and opportunities, and making informed decisions that drive long-term success.

The future is not a single destination, but a multitude of possibilities. Scenario planning allows us to explore these possibilities, prepare for uncertainties, and make informed decisions that can withstand the test of time. Remember, the best way to predict the future is to create it.

EIGHT

DECISION MATRIX: EVALUATING OPTIONS OBJECTIVELY AND CHOOSING THE BEST PATH.

In the intricate landscape of decision-making, where choices often carry significant consequences, the pursuit of objectivity and informed judgment is paramount. A decision matrix emerges as a valuable tool, providing a structured framework for evaluating options and selecting the most optimal path. By systematically assessing alternatives against a set of predetermined criteria, decision-makers can navigate complex choices with clarity and confidence, ensuring that their decisions are rooted in logic and aligned with their goals.

At its core, a decision matrix is a visual representation of various options and their respective attributes. It is a table-like structure where rows represent the different alternatives under consideration, and columns represent the criteria upon which these alternatives will be evaluated. Each cell within the matrix contains a rating or score that reflects how well each alternative performs against a specific criterion. This quantitative approach allows for a more objective comparison of options, reducing the influence of personal biases and emotional factors that can cloud judgment.

The criteria used in a decision matrix can vary depending on the nature of the decision being made. For example, when choosing a new supplier, the criteria might include cost, quality, delivery time, and reliability. When selecting a new marketing strategy, the criteria might include reach, engagement, conversion rate, and return on investment. The key is to choose criteria that are relevant, measurable, and aligned with the organization's overall goals.

Once the criteria have been established, the next step is to assign weights to each criterion. This reflects the relative importance of each criterion in the overall decision. For example, if cost is the most important factor in choosing a new supplier, it would be assigned a higher weight than delivery time. The weights can be determined through various methods, such as pairwise comparison or expert judgment.

With the criteria and weights in place, the decision matrix is ready to be populated. This involves assigning a rating or score to each alternative for each criterion. The ratings can be numerical, such as a scale of 1 to 5, or qualitative, such as "high," "medium," or "low." The ratings should be based on objective data and analysis, whenever possible.

Once the matrix is populated, the final step is to calculate a weighted score for each alternative. This is done by multiplying the rating for each criterion by its corresponding weight and summing the results across all criteria. The alternative with the highest weighted score is considered the most optimal choice, based on the criteria and weights that were established.

The decision matrix offers several key advantages. First, it provides a structured and systematic approach to decision-making, ensuring that all relevant factors are considered. This can help to reduce the risk of overlooking important information or making impulsive decisions. Second, the decision matrix promotes objectivity by quantifying the evaluation of alternatives. This can help to reduce the influence of personal biases and emotional factors that can cloud judgment. Third, the decision matrix facilitates communication and collaboration by providing a visual representation of the decision-making process. This can help to ensure that all stakeholders are on the same page and that the final decision is supported by a clear and logical rationale.

However, the decision matrix is not without its limitations. It relies on the accuracy and relevance of the criteria and weights that are used. If the criteria are poorly chosen or the weights are inaccurate, the resulting decision may be suboptimal. Additionally, the decision matrix can be time-consuming to create and may not be suitable for all types of decisions. For example, it may not be appropriate for decisions that are highly subjective or that involve a high degree of uncertainty.

Despite these limitations, the decision matrix remains a valuable tool for evaluating options and choosing the best path. By providing a structured framework for decision-making, it can help organizations to make more informed, objective, and confident choices. This can lead to better outcomes, improved performance, and increased success in the long run.

In conclusion, the decision matrix is a powerful tool for navigating the complexities of decision-making. By systematically assessing alternatives against a set of predetermined criteria, it empowers decision-makers to choose the most optimal path with clarity and confidence. While it is not without its limitations, the decision matrix remains a valuable asset for any organization that seeks to make informed, objective, and successful decisions.

ᕐᕐᕐ

Decisions shape our destiny. The decision matrix provides a structured approach to evaluating options objectively and choosing the best path forward. By considering multiple criteria and their relative importance, we can make confident choices that align with our goals.

NINE

MIND MAPPING: VISUALIZING CONNECTIONS AND UNLOCKING NEW IDEAS.

In the intricate dance of human thought, ideas often emerge as fleeting sparks, interconnected yet seemingly disparate. To harness the full potential of these ideas, a visual tool known as mind mapping has emerged as a powerful ally. Mind mapping is a versatile technique that allows individuals and teams to capture, organize, and visualize their thoughts in a non-linear and intuitive manner. By creating a visual representation of ideas and their relationships, mind mapping unlocks the hidden connections between concepts, fostering creativity, enhancing understanding, and paving the way for innovative solutions.

At its core, mind mapping is a graphical representation of information. It typically starts with a central idea or topic, represented by a word or image in the center of a page. From this central node, branches radiate outwards, each representing a subtopic or related idea. These branches can then be further subdivided into smaller branches, creating a hierarchical structure that reflects the relationships between different concepts.

Unlike traditional linear note-taking methods, mind mapping encourages a more organic and free-flowing approach to capturing information. Instead of writing in sentences or paragraphs, ideas are expressed in keywords, phrases, or images. This allows for greater flexibility and creativity, as individuals can capture their thoughts in a way that feels natural and intuitive to them.

The visual nature of mind maps is a key factor in their effectiveness. By presenting information in a graphical format, mind maps tap into the brain's natural ability to process visual information. This makes it easier to understand complex concepts, identify patterns and relationships, and remember information. For example, a mind map of a business plan might reveal connections between different aspects of the plan that were not immediately apparent in a linear text format.

Mind mapping is a versatile tool that can be used for a wide range of purposes. It can be used for brainstorming, note-taking, planning, problem-solving, and decision-making. It can also be used for learning, as it can help to visualize the relationships between different concepts and make complex information more accessible.

In the context of business, mind mapping can be a valuable tool for generating new ideas and solving problems. By visualizing the relationships between different concepts, mind maps can help teams to identify potential solutions that might not have been apparent otherwise. For example, a mind map of a customer service issue might reveal underlying causes that could be addressed to improve customer satisfaction.

Mind mapping can also be used to improve communication and collaboration. By creating a shared visual representation of a project or problem, teams can ensure that everyone is on the same page and working towards the same goals. Mind maps can also be used to facilitate brainstorming sessions, as they provide a visual framework for generating and organizing ideas.

In addition to its practical applications, mind mapping can also have a positive impact on cognitive function. Studies have shown that mind mapping can improve memory, focus, and creativity. It can also help to reduce stress and anxiety by providing a structured way to process information and make decisions.

The benefits of mind mapping are numerous. It is a simple yet powerful tool that can be used by individuals and teams to improve productivity, creativity, and communication. By visualizing connections and unlocking new ideas, mind mapping can help businesses to solve problems, make decisions, and achieve their goals.

There are many different ways to create a mind map. Some people prefer to use pen and paper, while others prefer to use software. There are also many different mind mapping styles, from simple radial maps to more complex hierarchical structures. The most important thing is to choose a method that works for you and that you find easy to use.

Here are a few tips for creating effective mind maps:

Start with a central idea or topic.

Use keywords, phrases, or images to represent ideas.

Connect related ideas with branches.

Use different colors and fonts to highlight important information.

Keep your mind map organized and easy to read.

Review and update your mind map regularly.

Mind mapping is a powerful tool that can be used to unlock the full potential of your ideas. By visualizing connections and exploring new possibilities, mind mapping can help you to achieve your goals and make a real impact in your business.

Our minds are vast landscapes of interconnected ideas. Mind mapping allows us to visualize these connections, unlocking new insights and sparking creativity. Don't be afraid to let your thoughts branch out and explore new territories.

TEN

STORYTELLING: HARNESSING THE POWER OF NARRATIVE TO ENGAGE AND INSPIRE.

In the vast landscape of human communication, storytelling stands as a timeless art form, a vessel for conveying ideas, emotions, and experiences that resonate deeply with our souls. From ancient myths and legends to modern-day marketing campaigns, stories have the power to captivate, inspire, and transform. In the realm of business, storytelling has emerged as a potent tool for engaging audiences, building brand loyalty, and driving meaningful change. By harnessing the power of narrative, organizations can connect with their customers, employees, and stakeholders on a deeper level, fostering trust, loyalty, and shared purpose.

Storytelling is more than just a collection of words and images; it is a fundamental human need. We are wired for stories, drawn to the emotional connection they create and the meaning they impart. Stories have the power to transport us to different worlds, introduce us to new perspectives, and challenge our assumptions. They can make us laugh, cry, and feel a whole range of emotions. This emotional connection is what makes storytelling so effective in engaging and inspiring audiences.

In the business world, storytelling can be used to achieve a variety of goals. It can be used to build brand awareness and create a strong brand identity. By sharing stories that reflect the company's values and mission, businesses can create a sense of authenticity and connect with their target audience on a deeper level. Storytelling can also be used to engage employees and foster a sense of belonging. By sharing stories that highlight the company's history, culture, and achievements, businesses can inspire their employees and create a shared sense of purpose.

Storytelling can also be used to drive sales and marketing efforts. By crafting compelling narratives that resonate with potential customers, businesses can generate interest in their products or services and drive sales. Storytelling can also be used to build relationships with customers and create a loyal following. By sharing stories that showcase the positive impact of their products or services, businesses can create a sense of community and build trust with their customers.

To harness the power of storytelling, businesses must first understand the key elements of a compelling narrative. A good story has a clear beginning, middle, and end. It has a protagonist who faces challenges and overcomes obstacles to achieve their goals. The story should also have a conflict or tension that keeps the audience engaged. Most importantly, the story should have a message or moral that resonates with the audience.

The most effective stories are those that evoke emotions in the audience. Whether it's joy, sadness, anger, or fear, emotions are what make stories memorable and impactful. By tapping into the emotional core of their audience, businesses can create stories that resonate on a deeper level and inspire action.

Authenticity is another crucial element of effective storytelling. Audiences can easily spot inauthentic or manipulative stories, so it's important for businesses to be genuine and transparent in their storytelling. This means sharing stories that are true to the company's values and mission, and avoiding stories that are overly promotional or self-serving.

The medium through which a story is told can also impact its effectiveness. While written stories can be powerful, visual storytelling through videos, images, and infographics can be even more impactful. Visual storytelling can capture the audience's attention and make the story more memorable. It can also be used to convey complex information in a more accessible and engaging way.

In today's digital age, social media platforms have become a powerful tool for storytelling. By sharing stories on platforms like Facebook, Instagram, and Twitter, businesses can reach a wider audience and engage with their customers in real-time. Social media also allows for two-way communication, enabling businesses to gather feedback from their audience and refine their storytelling approach.

Storytelling is not just for large corporations with big marketing budgets. Small businesses and startups can also harness the power of storytelling to build their brand and connect with their customers. By sharing stories that highlight their unique value proposition, small businesses can differentiate themselves from the competition and create a loyal following.

In conclusion, storytelling is a powerful tool that can be used to engage and inspire audiences, build brand loyalty, and drive meaningful change. By understanding the key elements of a compelling narrative, evoking emotions, and maintaining authenticity, businesses can create stories that resonate with their target audience and achieve their desired outcomes. Whether it's through written stories, visual storytelling, or social media, the power of narrative can unlock new opportunities and drive success in the modern business landscape. By embracing the art of storytelling, organizations can create a lasting impact on their customers, employees, and stakeholders, and build a brand that stands the test of time.

Stories are the universal language of the human experience. By harnessing the power of narrative, we can engage, inspire, and connect with our audience on a deeper level. Remember, the most effective stories are those that evoke emotions and convey a meaningful message.

ELEVEN

GAMIFICATION: TRANSFORMING WORK INTO PLAY TO BOOST MOTIVATION AND ENGAGEMENT.

In the quest for enhanced productivity, motivation, and engagement within the workplace, a novel approach has emerged, drawing inspiration from an unlikely source: games. Gamification, the application of game-design elements and principles in non-game contexts, has proven to be a transformative force, breathing new life into mundane tasks and fostering a more enjoyable and rewarding work environment. By tapping into the intrinsic human desire for challenge, achievement, and recognition, gamification can unlock the hidden potential within individuals and teams, leading to remarkable results.

At its core, gamification is about understanding what makes games so engaging and applying those same principles to other areas of life, including work. Games often involve clear goals, immediate feedback, rewards for progress, and a sense of competition or collaboration. These elements tap into our natural instincts for mastery, autonomy, and social connection, making the experience inherently enjoyable and motivating.

One of the key benefits of gamification is its ability to increase motivation. When tasks are framed as challenges or quests, individuals are more likely to feel a sense of ownership and investment in their work. The introduction of rewards, such as points, badges, or levels, provides a tangible sense of progress and achievement, further fueling motivation. This can be particularly effective for repetitive or mundane tasks that might otherwise feel demotivating.

Gamification can also enhance engagement by making work more fun and interactive. By incorporating elements of play, such as quizzes, puzzles, or simulations, gamification can transform even the most tedious tasks into enjoyable experiences. This not only makes work more enjoyable but also promotes deeper learning and understanding. When employees are engaged in their work, they are more likely to be productive, creative, and innovative.

Another advantage of gamification is its ability to foster a sense of community and collaboration. By introducing leaderboards, team challenges, or social features, gamification can encourage employees to interact with each other, share knowledge, and work together towards common goals. This can lead to a more positive and supportive work environment, where employees feel connected to their colleagues and invested in the success of the team.

Gamification can also be used to provide personalized learning and development opportunities. By tailoring challenges and rewards to individual needs and preferences, gamification can help employees develop new skills, knowledge, and competencies in a way that is both engaging and effective. This can lead to increased job satisfaction, improved performance, and greater career development opportunities.

Despite its numerous benefits, gamification is not without its challenges. One of the main criticisms of gamification is that it can be perceived as manipulative or exploitative. If not implemented thoughtfully, gamification can feel like a thinly veiled attempt to control or manipulate employees. To avoid this pitfall, it is important to ensure that gamification is used ethically and transparently, with clear goals and expectations.

Another challenge is that gamification may not be suitable for all tasks or all individuals. Some tasks may be too complex or sensitive to be gamified effectively, and some individuals may not respond well to game-like elements. Therefore, it is important to carefully consider the context and audience before implementing gamification.

To ensure the successful implementation of gamification, it is essential to follow a few key principles. First, it is important to align the game mechanics with the desired outcomes. The gamification elements should be designed to support the organization's goals and values, not just to make work more fun. Second, it is important to create a clear and transparent system that is easy to understand and navigate. Employees should know what is expected of them and how their performance will be rewarded. Third, it is important to provide regular feedback and recognition. This can be done through leaderboards, badges, or other forms of public acknowledgment. Finally, it is important to keep the game fresh and engaging by introducing new challenges and rewards on a regular basis.

Gamification has the potential to revolutionize the workplace by transforming work into play. By tapping into the intrinsic human desire for challenge, achievement, and recognition, gamification can boost motivation, engagement, and productivity. However, it is important to implement gamification thoughtfully and ethically, ensuring that it aligns with the organization's goals and values. With careful planning and execution, gamification can create a more enjoyable, rewarding, and productive work environment for everyone.

ϷϷϷ

Work doesn't have to be a chore. Gamification transforms mundane tasks into engaging challenges, boosting motivation and productivity. By incorporating elements of play, we can tap into our intrinsic desire for achievement and create a more enjoyable work environment.

TWELVE
COLLABORATION: LEVERAGING COLLECTIVE INTELLIGENCE FOR BETTER RESULTS.

In the intricate dance of human progress, collaboration has emerged as a driving force, a testament to the power of collective intelligence. From the earliest hunter-gatherer societies to modern-day corporations, the ability to work together towards a common goal has been a defining characteristic of our species.

In the realm of business, collaboration has become increasingly crucial in an era of complex challenges and rapid change.

By leveraging the diverse skills, knowledge, and perspectives of individuals and teams, organizations can unlock a wealth of creative potential, enhance problem-solving capabilities, and achieve remarkable results that surpass the limitations of individual efforts.

Collaboration, at its essence, is the act of working together to achieve a shared objective. It involves the pooling of resources, the sharing of information, and the coordination of efforts. Collaboration can take many forms, from informal brainstorming sessions to formal partnerships and alliances. Regardless of the specific form it takes, collaboration is rooted in the belief that the whole is greater than the sum of its parts.

One of the key benefits of collaboration is the ability to leverage collective intelligence. This refers to the shared knowledge, skills, and experiences of a group of individuals.

When people collaborate, they bring their unique perspectives and insights to the table, creating a pool of knowledge that is far greater than any one individual could possess.

This collective intelligence can be used to solve complex problems, generate innovative ideas, and make better decisions.

In the business world, collaboration can take many forms. It can occur within teams, between departments, across organizations, and even across industries. For example, a cross-functional team might collaborate to develop a new product, while different departments might collaborate to streamline a process.

Collaboration can also occur between businesses and their customers, suppliers, or partners. For instance, a company might collaborate with its customers to co-create new products or services.

The benefits of collaboration are numerous. Collaboration can lead to increased innovation, as diverse perspectives and ideas are brought together. It can also lead to improved problem-solving, as teams can leverage their collective intelligence to find creative solutions. Collaboration can also foster trust and build relationships, creating a more positive and productive work environment.

Despite its many benefits, collaboration is not without its challenges. One of the main challenges is overcoming the barriers to communication and cooperation. These barriers can include differences in language, culture, values, and goals.

They can also include logistical challenges, such as geographic distance or time zone differences. To overcome these barriers, it is important to establish clear communication channels, foster a culture of trust and respect, and use technology to facilitate collaboration.

Another challenge is managing conflict. When people with different perspectives and ideas come together, conflict is inevitable. However, conflict can be a positive force if it is managed effectively. By encouraging open communication, active listening, and compromise, teams can leverage conflict to generate new ideas and find creative solutions.

To foster collaboration, organizations can implement a variety of strategies. One strategy is to create a culture that values collaboration. This can be done by encouraging teamwork, recognizing and rewarding collaboration, and providing opportunities for employees to learn and develop their collaboration skills. Another strategy is to provide the necessary tools and resources to support collaboration. This can include collaboration software, online meeting tools, and shared workspaces.

In conclusion, collaboration is a powerful tool for leveraging collective intelligence and achieving better results. By working together, individuals and teams can tap into a wealth of knowledge, skills, and perspectives, leading to increased innovation, improved problem-solving, and a more positive and productive work environment.

While collaboration is not without its challenges, the benefits far outweigh the costs. By fostering a culture of collaboration and providing the necessary tools and resources, organizations can unlock the full potential of their workforce and achieve remarkable results.

ᗡᗡᗡ

Collaboration is not just about working together; it's about leveraging collective intelligence to achieve extraordinary results. When we combine our diverse skills, knowledge, and perspectives, we can overcome challenges and unlock new possibilities. Remember, the whole is greater than the sum of its parts.

THIRTEEN

EXPERIMENTATION: EMBRACING FAILURE AS A LEARNING OPPORTUNITY.

In the intricate dance of innovation and progress, experimentation emerges as a cornerstone, a dynamic process that propels us beyond the familiar and into the realm of the unknown. It is a journey marked by curiosity, exploration, and the courage to venture into uncharted territories. Yet, inherent within experimentation lies the specter of failure, a prospect that often evokes fear and aversion. However, true innovators understand that failure is not an ending but rather a stepping stone, a valuable learning opportunity that paves the way for future success.

Experimentation, at its core, is the act of testing a hypothesis or trying out a new approach to see if it yields the desired results. It is a process of trial and error, where mistakes are not only inevitable but also essential for learning and growth. In the words of Thomas Edison, "I have not failed. I've just found 10,000 ways that won't work." This perspective highlights the importance of embracing failure as an integral part of the experimentation process.

The fear of failure is a natural human instinct. We are wired to avoid pain and seek pleasure, and failure can often be associated with negative emotions such as disappointment, shame, and embarrassment. However, in the context of experimentation, failure should not be viewed as a personal shortcoming but rather as a valuable source of information. Each failed experiment provides insights into what doesn't work, allowing us to refine our approach and move closer to a successful outcome.

Embracing failure as a learning opportunity requires a shift in mindset. Instead of viewing failure as a setback, we need to reframe it as a valuable feedback mechanism. This means analyzing the reasons for the failure, identifying the lessons learned, and applying those lessons to future experiments. By adopting a growth mindset, we can view failure as a stepping stone on the path to success, rather than a roadblock.

In the business world, experimentation is essential for innovation and growth. Companies that are willing to experiment are more likely to discover new products, services, and processes that can give them a competitive edge. However, experimentation also carries risks. Failed experiments can be costly and time-consuming, and they can damage morale if not handled properly.

To mitigate the risks of experimentation, it is important to create a culture that encourages and supports experimentation. This means creating a safe space where employees feel comfortable taking risks and trying new things. It also means providing the necessary resources and support to enable employees to learn from their mistakes and move forward.

One way to foster a culture of experimentation is to celebrate failures as well as successes. By recognizing and rewarding employees who are willing to take risks and learn from their mistakes, organizations can create a positive feedback loop that encourages more experimentation. This can lead to a more innovative and adaptable workforce that is better equipped to handle the challenges of the modern business environment.

Another way to encourage experimentation is to create a learning environment where employees can share their experiences and learn from each other's mistakes. This can be done through regular debriefing sessions, knowledge-sharing platforms, and mentorship programs. By fostering a culture of learning, organizations can create a continuous cycle of experimentation and improvement.

Experimentation is not just about trying new things; it is also about measuring and analyzing the results. To learn from experiments, it is essential to track the outcomes, identify the factors that contributed to success or failure, and use this information to inform future decisions. This requires a data-driven approach to experimentation, where hypotheses are tested and results are analyzed systematically.

In conclusion, experimentation is a critical component of innovation and progress. It is a process of exploration, discovery, and learning. While failure is an inevitable part of experimentation, it should not be feared but embraced as a valuable learning opportunity. By fostering a culture of experimentation, organizations can unlock the creative potential of their employees, drive innovation, and achieve long-term success.

$$\wp\wp\wp$$

Failure is not the opposite of success; it's a stepping stone on the path to it. By embracing experimentation and learning from our mistakes, we can continuously improve and innovate. Remember, the only true failure is the failure to learn.

FOURTEEN

PROTOTYPING: BUILDING QUICK, ITERATIVE MODELS TO TEST AND REFINE IDEAS.

In the ever-evolving landscape of innovation, the journey from concept to reality is often fraught with uncertainty and risk. The leap from a brilliant idea to a tangible product or service can be daunting, and the fear of investing significant time and resources into a flawed concept can be paralyzing. To bridge this gap and mitigate risks, the invaluable practice of prototyping has emerged as a cornerstone of the innovation process. Prototyping, the art of building quick, iterative models to test and refine ideas, empowers creators to transform abstract concepts into tangible forms, gather feedback, and iteratively improve their designs before committing to full-scale development.

Prototyping is, in essence, a process of learning by doing. It involves creating simplified representations of a product or service, often using readily available materials or digital tools, to explore different design options, test functionality, and gather user feedback. Prototypes can range in fidelity from low-fidelity mockups, such as sketches or paper models, to high-fidelity interactive prototypes that closely resemble the final product.

The primary goal of prototyping is to validate and refine ideas before investing significant resources in full-scale development. By creating tangible representations of their concepts, creators can gain valuable insights into the feasibility, usability, and desirability of their ideas. Prototypes allow them to test assumptions, identify potential flaws or shortcomings, and gather feedback from potential users or stakeholders. This iterative process of building, testing, and refining helps to de-risk the innovation process and increase the likelihood of success.

Prototyping also plays a crucial role in communication and collaboration. A prototype can serve as a common reference point for team members, stakeholders, and potential users, facilitating discussions, clarifying expectations, and aligning everyone on a shared vision. By visualizing the concept in a tangible form, prototypes can bridge the gap between abstract ideas and concrete realities, making it easier for everyone involved to understand and contribute to the design process.

There are numerous types of prototypes, each serving a different purpose and offering unique advantages. Low-fidelity prototypes, such as sketches, wireframes, or storyboards, are quick and inexpensive to create, making them ideal for early-stage exploration and ideation. They allow designers to rapidly generate and test a wide range of ideas without getting bogged down in details.

As the design process progresses, creators can move on to medium-fidelity prototypes, such as 3D models, interactive mockups, or role-playing scenarios. These prototypes offer a more detailed representation of the concept, allowing for more in-depth testing of functionality, usability, and user experience. Medium-fidelity prototypes can also be used to gather feedback from potential users, helping to identify areas for improvement and refine the design.

High-fidelity prototypes, such as functional prototypes or beta versions, closely resemble the final product and are used for final testing and validation. They allow creators to assess the overall performance, functionality, and user experience of the product in a real-world setting. High-fidelity prototypes can also be used to gather feedback from stakeholders, secure funding, or generate pre-launch buzz.

The choice of prototyping method depends on various factors, such as the stage of development, the complexity of the concept, the available resources, and the desired level of fidelity. The key is to choose a method that is appropriate for the specific needs of the project and that allows for rapid iteration and feedback.

Prototyping is an iterative process, and it is important to embrace failure as a learning opportunity. Not all prototypes will be successful, and that is perfectly normal. In fact, failed prototypes can be just as valuable as successful ones, as they provide valuable insights into what doesn't work and help to refine the design. The key is to learn from each iteration, incorporate feedback, and continuously improve the prototype until it meets the desired goals.

In conclusion, prototyping is an indispensable tool for transforming ideas into reality. By building quick, iterative models to test and refine concepts, creators can de-risk the innovation process, gather valuable feedback, and increase the likelihood of success. Prototyping fosters communication and collaboration, allowing teams to align on a shared vision and work together towards a common goal. Whether it's a low-fidelity mockup or a high-fidelity interactive prototype, the act of creating tangible representations of ideas empowers creators to explore, experiment, and ultimately bring their visions to life.

ϸϸϸ

Prototyping is the bridge between ideas and reality. By building quick, iterative models, we can test our assumptions, gather feedback, and refine our designs before committing to full-scale development. Remember, the best way to learn is by doing.

FIFTEEN

Agile Development: Adapting to Change and Delivering Value Incrementally.

In the fast-paced and ever-changing landscape of modern business, the ability to adapt to change and deliver value quickly is paramount. Traditional project management methodologies, with their rigid plans and long development cycles, often struggle to keep up with the demands of today's dynamic markets. Enter Agile Development, a revolutionary approach to project management that prioritizes flexibility, collaboration, and continuous improvement. By breaking down projects into smaller, manageable increments and delivering value iteratively, Agile Development enables organizations to respond to change quickly, adapt to evolving customer needs, and achieve a competitive advantage.

At its core, Agile Development is a mindset that embraces change as an opportunity rather than a threat. It is a philosophy that permeates every aspect of the project, from planning and execution to delivery and feedback. The Agile Manifesto, a set of guiding principles for Agile software development, emphasizes individuals and interactions over processes and tools, working software over comprehensive documentation, customer collaboration over contract negotiation, and responding to change over following a plan.

The Agile Development process is characterized by short iterations, or sprints, typically lasting one to four weeks. During each sprint, a cross-functional team works together to deliver a potentially shippable product increment. This iterative approach allows for frequent feedback and adaptation, ensuring that the final product meets the needs of the customer and the market.

One of the key benefits of Agile Development is its ability to adapt to change. In traditional project management, changes to requirements or scope can be costly and time-consuming to implement. In Agile Development, change is expected and embraced. The iterative nature of the process allows for regular feedback and adjustments, ensuring that the project remains on track and aligned with the evolving needs of the customer.

Agile Development also emphasizes customer collaboration. Throughout the project, the customer is actively involved in providing feedback, prioritizing features, and making decisions. This collaborative approach ensures that the final product meets the customer's needs and expectations.

Another advantage of Agile Development is its focus on delivering value incrementally. Instead of waiting until the end of the project to deliver a finished product, Agile teams deliver working software in short iterations. This allows the customer to realize value early on and provides opportunities for feedback and improvement throughout the development process.

Agile Development also promotes a culture of continuous improvement. Teams regularly reflect on their work, identify areas for improvement, and implement changes to their processes. This iterative learning process allows teams to become more efficient and effective over time.

Agile Development has been successfully implemented in a wide range of industries, from software development to marketing, manufacturing, and even government. In software development, Agile has become the dominant methodology, enabling teams to deliver high-quality software faster and more efficiently. In other industries, Agile has been used to improve project outcomes, increase customer satisfaction, and reduce costs.

Despite its proven success, Agile Development is not without its challenges. It requires a shift in mindset and culture, as well as a commitment to collaboration and continuous improvement. Organizations may need to invest in training and resources to support the implementation process. Additionally, Agile Development may not be suitable for all types of projects, particularly those with fixed deadlines or budgets.

However, the benefits of Agile Development far outweigh the challenges. By prioritizing flexibility, collaboration, and continuous improvement, Agile enables organizations to respond to change quickly, adapt to evolving customer needs, and deliver value incrementally. This can lead to improved project outcomes, increased customer satisfaction, and a stronger competitive position in the market.

In conclusion, Agile Development is a revolutionary approach to project management that has transformed the way organizations operate. By breaking down projects into smaller, manageable increments and delivering value iteratively, Agile enables organizations to respond to change quickly, adapt to evolving customer needs, and achieve a competitive advantage. While it requires a shift in mindset and culture, the benefits of Agile far outweigh the challenges, making it an essential tool for any organization that seeks to thrive in today's dynamic and fast-paced business environment.

❦❦❦

In the fast-paced world of business, agility is key. Agile development allows us to adapt to change, deliver value incrementally, and continuously improve our products and services. Remember, the ability to adapt is what sets successful businesses apart.

SIXTEEN

Data-Driven Decision Making: Using insights to inform and optimize choices.

In the digital age, where information flows like a torrent, the ability to harness and interpret data has become a defining factor in the success of businesses across industries. Data-driven decision making, a methodology that emphasizes the use of facts, metrics, and analysis to guide strategic choices, has emerged as a cornerstone of modern management.

By leveraging the insights gleaned from data, organizations can gain a deeper understanding of their operations, customers, and markets, enabling them to make informed decisions that drive growth, efficiency, and innovation.

At its core, data-driven decision making is about replacing gut feeling and intuition with evidence-based insights. It involves collecting, analyzing, and interpreting data from various sources to gain a comprehensive understanding of the situation at hand.

This data can come from internal sources, such as sales figures, customer surveys, and employee feedback, as well as external sources, such as market research reports, social media analytics, and economic indicators.

The rise of big data and advanced analytics has further amplified the power of data-driven decision making. With the ability to process vast amounts of data in real time, organizations can now uncover patterns, trends, and correlations that were previously hidden. This allows them to make more accurate predictions, identify emerging opportunities, and mitigate potential risks.

The benefits of data-driven decision making are numerous. First and foremost, it improves the quality of decisions. By basing decisions on facts and evidence, organizations can reduce the risk of making costly mistakes based on faulty assumptions or biases. Data-driven decisions are more likely to be objective, rational, and aligned with the organization's goals.

Second, data-driven decision making can lead to increased efficiency and productivity. By analyzing data on processes and performance, organizations can identify bottlenecks, inefficiencies, and areas for improvement. This can lead to the optimization of workflows, the reduction of waste, and the allocation of resources more effectively.

Third, data-driven decision making can enhance customer satisfaction and loyalty. By analyzing customer data, organizations can gain insights into their preferences, behaviors, and pain points. This allows them to tailor their products, services, and marketing messages to meet the specific needs of their customers, resulting in higher levels of satisfaction and loyalty.

Fourth, data-driven decision making can drive innovation. By analyzing data on market trends, emerging technologies, and customer needs, organizations can identify new opportunities for growth and innovation. This can lead to the development of new products, services, or business models that can give them a competitive edge.

However, data-driven decision making is not without its challenges. One of the main challenges is the sheer volume of data that is available. Organizations need to have the right tools and expertise to collect, store, and analyze this data effectively. They also need to ensure that the data is accurate, reliable, and relevant to the decisions being made.

Another challenge is the need for a cultural shift. Data-driven decision making requires a willingness to embrace change and challenge traditional ways of thinking. It also requires a commitment to transparency and accountability, as decisions are based on evidence rather than gut feeling or personal opinions.

To overcome these challenges, organizations need to adopt a holistic approach to data-driven decision making. This involves investing in the right technology, building a data-savvy workforce, and fostering a culture that values data and evidence-based insights.

It also involves establishing clear processes for collecting, analyzing, and interpreting data, as well as mechanisms for communicating and acting on the insights gleaned from the data.

In conclusion, data-driven decision making is a powerful tool that can transform the way organizations operate. By leveraging the insights gleaned from data, organizations can make more informed decisions, improve efficiency, enhance customer satisfaction, and drive innovation.

While it requires a significant investment in technology, skills, and culture change, the benefits of data-driven decision making far outweigh the costs. As the world becomes increasingly data-driven, organizations that embrace this approach will be well-positioned for success in the digital age.

❧❧❧

Data is the language of the digital age. By harnessing the power of data-driven decision-making, we can gain valuable insights, make informed choices, and optimize our strategies. Remember, data is not just information; it's the key to unlocking your full potential.

SEVENTEEN

CUSTOMER JOURNEY MAPPING: UNDERSTANDING CUSTOMER NEEDS AND PAIN POINTS.

In the intricate dance of business success, the customer reigns supreme. Understanding their needs, desires, and pain points is not merely a strategic advantage but an imperative for sustained growth and relevance. This is where the powerful tool of Customer Journey Mapping (CJM) comes into play. CJM is a visual representation of the customer's experience with a product, service, or brand, from the initial point of contact to the final interaction. By meticulously tracing the customer's steps, emotions, and touchpoints, businesses can gain profound insights into their needs and pain points, enabling them to tailor their offerings and create a truly customer-centric experience.

At its core, CJM is a storytelling tool, a narrative that unfolds the customer's journey through various stages of interaction with a company. It is a visual map that outlines the touchpoints, actions, emotions, and motivations that define the customer experience. This map serves as a roadmap, guiding businesses towards a deeper understanding of their customers' needs and aspirations. By stepping into the shoes of their customers, businesses can identify areas for improvement, enhance customer satisfaction, and build lasting loyalty.

The process of creating a CJM begins with defining the scope and objectives of the map. This involves identifying the specific customer segment or persona that the map will focus on. It is crucial to choose a well-defined target audience, as different customer segments may have distinct needs and expectations. Once the scope is established, the next step is to gather data from various sources, such as customer surveys, interviews, website analytics, and social media interactions. This data provides valuable insights into the customer's behavior, preferences, and pain points.

With the data in hand, the next step is to map out the customer journey. This involves identifying the various stages of the customer's interaction with the company, from awareness and consideration to purchase and post-purchase. Each stage is then analyzed in detail, outlining the touchpoints, actions, emotions, and motivations that characterize the customer's experience.

Touchpoints are the specific interactions that the customer has with the company, such as visiting a website, calling customer service, or interacting with a salesperson. By identifying these touchpoints, businesses can understand how customers engage with their brand and pinpoint potential areas for improvement. Actions refer to the specific steps that customers take during their journey, such as browsing products, adding items to their cart, or completing a purchase. Analyzing these actions can reveal bottlenecks or friction points in the customer journey, allowing businesses to streamline their processes and enhance the overall experience.

Emotions play a crucial role in the customer journey. By understanding the emotions that customers experience at each stage, businesses can tailor their interactions to create a positive and memorable experience. For example, if customers are feeling frustrated or confused during a particular stage, businesses can provide additional support or information to alleviate their concerns.

Motivations are the underlying reasons why customers take certain actions or make certain decisions. By understanding these motivations, businesses can design their offerings to appeal to the specific needs and desires of their customers. For example, if customers are motivated by convenience, businesses can offer online ordering and fast delivery options.

Pain points are the specific challenges or frustrations that customers encounter during their journey. By identifying these pain points, businesses can proactively address them and improve the overall customer experience. For example, if customers are struggling to find the information they need on a website, businesses can redesign their website to make it more user-friendly.

Once the customer journey map is complete, the next step is to analyze the data and identify opportunities for improvement. This involves looking for patterns and trends in the customer data, as well as identifying areas where the customer experience falls short. The goal is to pinpoint specific actions that the business can take to enhance the customer journey and create a more positive and memorable experience.

The insights gleaned from the customer journey map can be used to inform a variety of business decisions. They can be used to improve marketing and sales efforts, optimize customer service interactions, and even redesign products or services. By understanding the customer's perspective, businesses can create a more customer-centric approach that resonates with their target audience and drives long-term loyalty.

Customer Journey Mapping is not a one-time exercise; it is an ongoing process that requires continuous monitoring and refinement. As customer needs and expectations evolve, businesses must adapt their strategies and offerings to stay relevant. By regularly reviewing and updating their customer journey maps, businesses can ensure that they are always meeting the needs of their customers and providing a superior experience.

In conclusion, Customer Journey Mapping is an invaluable tool for understanding customer needs and pain points. By meticulously tracing the customer's steps, emotions, and touchpoints, businesses can gain profound insights into their needs and aspirations. This understanding can then be used to inform business decisions, enhance customer satisfaction, and build lasting loyalty. By embracing a customer-centric approach and utilizing the power of Customer Journey Mapping, businesses can create a truly memorable and impactful customer experience that drives long-term success.

ppp

The customer journey is a story waiting to be told. By mapping out the customer experience, we can understand their needs, pain points, and motivations, and tailor our offerings to create a truly customer-centric experience. Remember, the customer is not just a buyer; they are the hero of your story.

EIGHTEEN

FEEDBACK LOOPS: CONTINUOUSLY IMPROVING THROUGH FEEDBACK AND ITERATION.

In the intricate dance of progress and innovation, feedback loops emerge as a powerful mechanism, a continuous cycle of learning and improvement that propels individuals, teams, and organizations towards excellence. Feedback loops, in essence, are systems where outputs are used as inputs for subsequent iterations, creating a virtuous cycle of refinement and growth. By actively seeking, analyzing, and acting upon feedback, individuals and organizations can identify areas for improvement, refine their strategies, and achieve sustainable success.

At its core, feedback is information about reactions to a product, a person's performance of a task, etc., used as a basis for improvement. It can be positive, highlighting strengths and successes, or negative, pointing out areas for improvement. Both types of feedback are essential for growth, as they provide valuable insights into what is working well and what needs to be adjusted.

Feedback loops can take many forms, depending on the context and the desired outcome. In a personal setting, feedback loops can involve seeking feedback from friends, family, or mentors on personal goals or behaviors. In a professional setting, feedback loops can involve seeking feedback from colleagues, managers, or customers on work performance or product development.

One of the key benefits of feedback loops is their ability to foster continuous improvement. By regularly seeking and acting upon feedback, individuals and organizations can identify areas where they are falling short and make necessary adjustments. This iterative process of learning and improvement can lead to significant gains in performance, productivity, and overall effectiveness.

In the business world, feedback loops are essential for staying ahead of the competition and meeting the evolving needs of customers. By gathering feedback from customers, businesses can identify areas where their products or services are falling short and make necessary improvements. This can lead to increased customer satisfaction, loyalty, and ultimately, profitability.

Feedback loops can also be used to improve internal processes and operations. By gathering feedback from employees, managers can identify bottlenecks, inefficiencies, and areas for improvement. This can lead to streamlined workflows, increased productivity, and a more positive and engaged workforce.

To create effective feedback loops, it is important to establish a culture of open communication and trust. Employees should feel safe and comfortable providing honest feedback, both positive and negative. Managers should be receptive to feedback and willing to act on it. This can involve creating formal feedback mechanisms, such as surveys, suggestion boxes, or regular performance reviews, as well as informal channels, such as one-on-one meetings or team discussions.

It is also important to ensure that feedback is specific, actionable, and timely. Vague or general feedback is not helpful, as it does not provide clear guidance on how to improve. Feedback should be actionable, meaning that it should provide specific suggestions or recommendations for improvement. And it should be timely, meaning that it should be provided as soon as possible after the behavior or performance in question.

In addition to seeking feedback from others, it is also important to engage in self-reflection and self-feedback. This involves taking a step back and honestly assessing one's own performance, strengths, and weaknesses. By reflecting on their own experiences and learning from their mistakes, individuals can continuously improve and grow.

Feedback loops are not a one-size-fits-all solution. The most effective feedback loops are those that are tailored to the specific needs and context of the individual or organization. For example, a feedback loop for a software development team might involve daily stand-up meetings, code reviews, and user testing, while a feedback loop for a sales team might involve weekly performance reviews, customer surveys, and win-loss analysis.

In conclusion, feedback loops are a powerful tool for continuous improvement. By actively seeking, analyzing, and acting upon feedback, individuals and organizations can identify areas for improvement, refine their strategies, and achieve sustainable success. Feedback loops foster a culture of learning and growth, where mistakes are viewed as opportunities for improvement and success is built on a foundation of continuous feedback and iteration. Whether it's in personal development, professional growth, or organizational performance, feedback loops are essential for unlocking our full potential and achieving our goals.

ᗁᗁᗁ

Feedback is the breakfast of champions. By creating continuous feedback loops, we can learn from our mistakes, refine our strategies, and continuously improve. Remember, feedback is not criticism; it's an opportunity for growth.

NINETEEN

INNOVATION CULTURE: FOSTERING AN ENVIRONMENT THAT EMBRACES CHANGE AND EXPERIMENTATION.

In the relentless pursuit of growth and competitive advantage, businesses are increasingly recognizing the importance of fostering an innovation culture. This is not merely a buzzword, but a fundamental shift in mindset, values, and practices that permeates every level of an organization. An innovation culture is a dynamic ecosystem where creativity thrives, experimentation is encouraged, and change is embraced as an opportunity rather than a threat. It is a breeding ground for new ideas, products, and services that can propel a company to new heights of success.

At its core, an innovation culture is characterized by a set of shared values and beliefs that prioritize creativity, risk-taking, and collaboration. It is an environment where employees feel empowered to challenge the status quo, experiment with new approaches, and share their ideas openly without fear of judgment or reprisal. This culture is not something that can be imposed from the top down; it must be nurtured and cultivated over time, with the active participation and commitment of everyone in the organization.

One of the key pillars of an innovation culture is the value placed on creativity. This means recognizing and rewarding employees who come up with new ideas, even if those ideas don't always pan out. It also means providing the resources and support that employees need to explore their creative potential, whether it's through training programs, brainstorming sessions, or access to new technologies.

Another important aspect of an innovation culture is the willingness to take risks. Innovation inherently involves stepping outside of one's comfort zone and trying new things. This can be scary, as there is always the possibility of failure. However, an innovation culture recognizes that failure is not the end of the road, but rather a valuable learning opportunity. By encouraging employees to take calculated risks and learn from their mistakes, organizations can foster a culture of continuous improvement and growth.

Collaboration is another essential element of an innovation culture. Innovation rarely happens in isolation; it is often the result of diverse perspectives and ideas coming together. An innovation culture encourages employees to work together across departments and disciplines, sharing their knowledge and expertise to solve complex problems and create new solutions. This can be facilitated through cross-functional teams, open communication channels, and collaborative workspaces.

Leadership plays a crucial role in fostering an innovation culture. Leaders who champion innovation, model risk-taking behavior, and create an environment where employees feel safe to experiment and fail are more likely to cultivate a culture of innovation. Leaders also need to provide the resources and support that employees need to bring their ideas to life, whether it's funding for research and development, access to prototyping tools, or the freedom to experiment with new approaches.

An innovation culture also requires a certain level of organizational flexibility. Traditional hierarchical structures and rigid processes can stifle creativity and innovation. Organizations that embrace an innovation culture are more likely to adopt flatter structures, empower employees to make decisions, and encourage experimentation. This can involve adopting agile methodologies, decentralizing decision-making, and promoting a culture of continuous learning and adaptation.

Fostering an innovation culture is not an overnight process; it takes time, effort, and commitment. However, the rewards are significant. Organizations with a strong innovation culture are more likely to attract and retain top talent, develop breakthrough products and services, and achieve sustainable growth. They are also better equipped to adapt to changing market conditions and stay ahead of the competition.

To cultivate an innovation culture, organizations can take a number of steps. First, they need to clearly articulate their innovation goals and communicate them to employees. This will help to create a shared understanding of what innovation means for the organization and how it aligns with the overall business strategy.

Second, organizations need to create an environment where employees feel safe to experiment and fail. This means providing the necessary resources and support, as well as fostering a culture of trust and openness. It also means celebrating failures as learning opportunities and rewarding employees who take risks.

Third, organizations need to encourage collaboration across departments and disciplines. This can be done through cross-functional teams, open communication channels, and collaborative workspaces. It also means breaking down silos and promoting a culture of knowledge sharing.

Fourth, organizations need to invest in employee development. This means providing training programs, mentorship opportunities, and access to new technologies. It also means creating a learning environment where employees can continuously develop their skills and knowledge.

Finally, organizations need to measure and track their progress towards their innovation goals. This will help to identify areas where they are succeeding and areas where they need to improve. It will also help to ensure that innovation remains a top priority for the organization.

In conclusion, fostering an innovation culture is a journey, not a destination. It requires a long-term commitment from leadership and the active participation of everyone in the organization. However, the rewards are significant. By embracing change and experimentation, organizations can unlock their creative potential, drive innovation, and achieve lasting success.

ppp

Innovation is not just about new ideas; it's about fostering a culture that embraces change and experimentation. By empowering employees to challenge the status quo and take risks, we can unlock a wealth of creative potential. Remember, innovation is a journey, not a destination.

TWENTY

DIVERSITY AND INCLUSION: HARNESSING THE POWER OF DIFFERENT PERSPECTIVES.

In the tapestry of human society, diversity is a vibrant thread, woven with the rich hues of varying backgrounds, experiences, and perspectives. This diversity, when embraced and nurtured, can become a wellspring of innovation, creativity, and resilience. In the realm of business, the concept of diversity and inclusion (D&I) has evolved from a moral imperative to a strategic advantage. Organizations that harness the power of different perspectives are not only fostering a more equitable and inclusive workplace but also unlocking a wealth of untapped potential that can drive growth, innovation, and success in an increasingly interconnected world.

Diversity, in its broadest sense, encompasses the variety of human experiences, including but not limited to race, ethnicity, gender, sexual orientation, age, disability, religion, and socioeconomic status. Each individual brings a unique set of perspectives, values, and beliefs shaped by their lived experiences. When these diverse perspectives are brought together, they create a rich tapestry of ideas, insights, and solutions that can propel an organization forward.

Inclusion, on the other hand, refers to the creation of a work environment where everyone feels valued, respected, and empowered to contribute their unique talents and perspectives. It is not enough to simply have a diverse workforce; organizations must also create a culture where everyone feels that they belong and their voices are heard. Inclusion is essential for harnessing the full potential of diversity, as it creates a sense of psychological safety that allows individuals to express their ideas freely and challenge the status quo.

The benefits of diversity and inclusion are numerous and far-reaching. Research has consistently shown that diverse teams are more innovative, creative, and adaptable than homogeneous teams. They are better able to solve complex problems, make sound decisions, and navigate through challenges. This is because diverse teams bring a wider range of perspectives, experiences, and skills to the table, allowing them to approach problems from different angles and consider a broader range of solutions.

In addition to enhancing problem-solving and decision-making capabilities, diversity and inclusion can also improve employee engagement and morale. When employees feel valued and included, they are more likely to be motivated, productive, and committed to their work. This can lead to increased retention rates, reduced absenteeism, and improved overall performance.

Diversity and inclusion can also enhance a company's reputation and brand image. In today's socially conscious marketplace, consumers are increasingly choosing to do business with companies that demonstrate a commitment to diversity and inclusion. A diverse and inclusive workforce can also help a company attract and retain top talent, as it signals that the company values diversity and is committed to creating an equitable and inclusive workplace.

Despite the clear benefits, creating a truly diverse and inclusive workplace is not without its challenges. Unconscious biases, stereotypes, and systemic barriers can all hinder progress towards a more inclusive workplace. To overcome these challenges, organizations must take a proactive and intentional approach to diversity and inclusion.

This can involve a variety of strategies, such as:

Setting clear diversity and inclusion goals: This involves defining specific targets for increasing representation of underrepresented groups at all levels of the organization.

Implementing diverse hiring practices: This can include blind recruitment, unconscious bias training, and targeted outreach to underrepresented groups.

Creating a culture of inclusion: This involves fostering a sense of belonging for all employees, regardless of their background or identity. This can be done through employee resource groups, diversity and inclusion training, and mentorship programs.

Holding leaders accountable: This means ensuring that diversity and inclusion are integrated into performance evaluations and that leaders are held accountable for creating a more inclusive workplace.

Measuring and tracking progress: This involves collecting data on diversity and inclusion metrics and using this data to track progress and identify areas for improvement.

By implementing these strategies, organizations can create a more diverse and inclusive workplace that harnesses the power of different perspectives to drive innovation, creativity, and success. However, it is important to remember that diversity and inclusion are not just about numbers; they are about creating a culture where everyone feels valued, respected, and empowered to contribute their unique talents and perspectives.

In conclusion, diversity and inclusion are essential for the success of any organization in today's globalized and interconnected world. By embracing the power of different perspectives, organizations can unlock a wealth of untapped potential, drive innovation, and achieve sustainable growth. Creating a truly diverse and inclusive workplace requires a long-term commitment and a multi-faceted approach. However, the benefits are clear, and the rewards are immense.

ᗑᗑᗑ

Diversity is not just a buzzword; it's a source of strength. By embracing diversity and inclusion, we can harness the power of different perspectives and create a more innovative, resilient, and successful organization. Remember, diversity is not just about fairness; it's about unlocking our full potential.

TWENTY-ONE

CHANGE MANAGEMENT: LEADING TEAMS THROUGH TRANSITIONS SMOOTHLY.

In the dynamic landscape of the modern world, change is the only constant. Organizations, like living organisms, must adapt and evolve to thrive in the face of shifting market trends, technological advancements, and unforeseen disruptions. Change, however, is not merely about implementing new strategies or adopting new technologies. It is about transforming the hearts and minds of the people who make up the organization. This is where change management, the art of leading teams through transitions smoothly, comes into play. Effective change management is not just about managing the technical aspects of change but also about addressing the human side of change, fostering buy-in, and ensuring a smooth and successful transition.

Change management is a structured approach to transitioning individuals, teams, and organizations from a current state to a desired future state. It involves a series of phases, from planning and preparation to implementation and reinforcement. Each phase requires careful consideration of the human element, as resistance to change is a natural human tendency. By understanding the psychological and emotional aspects of change, organizations can develop strategies to mitigate resistance, build support, and ensure that the change is embraced by everyone involved.

The first step in change management is to create a compelling vision for the future. This vision should clearly articulate the reasons for the change, the benefits it will bring, and the desired outcomes. A well-articulated vision can inspire and motivate employees, giving them a sense of purpose and direction. It can also help to align everyone around a common goal, creating a sense of unity and shared purpose.

Once the vision is established, the next step is to communicate the change effectively. This involves providing clear and transparent information about the change, its implications, and the timeline for implementation. Communication should be ongoing and multi-directional, allowing for questions, concerns, and feedback. It is important to address any rumors or misinformation that may arise, as these can fuel resistance and undermine the change effort.

In addition to communication, it is crucial to engage employees in the change process. This can be done through various means, such as involving employees in decision-making, seeking their input and feedback, and providing opportunities for training and development. When employees feel that they have a voice in the change process, they are more likely to embrace it and become advocates for it.

Another important aspect of change management is addressing resistance. Resistance to change is a natural human response, often driven by fear of the unknown, loss of control, or perceived threats to one's job or status. To mitigate resistance, it is important to acknowledge and validate employees' concerns, provide support and resources to help them adapt to the change, and celebrate small wins along the way.

Building a coalition of support is also crucial for successful change management. This involves identifying and engaging key stakeholders who can champion the change and influence others to embrace it. These stakeholders can include senior leaders, managers, influential employees, and external partners. By building a strong coalition of support, organizations can create a sense of momentum and overcome resistance.

The implementation phase of change management is where the rubber meets the road. This is where the actual changes are put into place and the organization begins to transition to the desired future state. During this phase, it is important to monitor progress closely, address any issues that arise, and communicate regularly with employees to keep them informed and engaged.

Once the change has been implemented, the final phase is reinforcement. This involves ensuring that the change is sustained over time and that employees continue to embrace it. This can be done through ongoing communication, training, and recognition of successes. It is also important to celebrate the achievements of the change effort and acknowledge the contributions of everyone involved.

Change management is a complex and challenging process, but it is essential for organizations to thrive in today's rapidly changing world. By understanding the human side of change and implementing effective change management strategies, organizations can navigate transitions smoothly, minimize disruptions, and achieve their desired outcomes. Effective change management is not just about managing the technical aspects of change but also about leading people through the emotional and psychological aspects of change. By fostering buy-in, building support, and celebrating successes, organizations can create a culture of change that embraces innovation, adaptability, and continuous improvement.

ᗠᗠᗠ

Change is inevitable, but it doesn't have to be disruptive. By implementing effective change management strategies, we can lead our teams through transitions smoothly, minimizing resistance and maximizing buy-in. Remember, change is not just about what we do; it's about how we do it.

TWENTY-TWO

CONTINUOUS LEARNING: STAYING AHEAD OF THE CURVE WITH NEW SKILLS AND KNOWLEDGE.

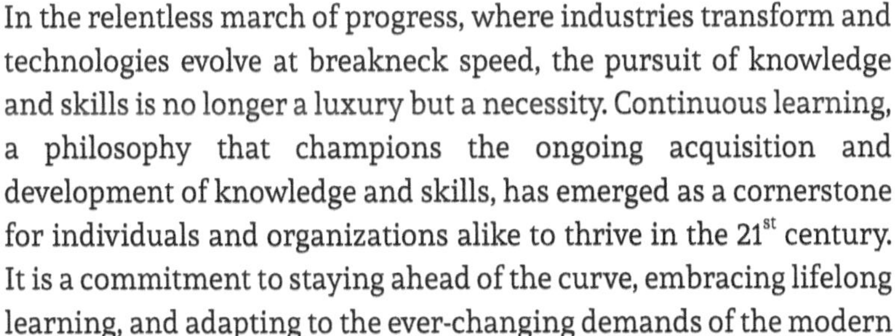

In the relentless march of progress, where industries transform and technologies evolve at breakneck speed, the pursuit of knowledge and skills is no longer a luxury but a necessity. Continuous learning, a philosophy that champions the ongoing acquisition and development of knowledge and skills, has emerged as a cornerstone for individuals and organizations alike to thrive in the 21st century. It is a commitment to staying ahead of the curve, embracing lifelong learning, and adapting to the ever-changing demands of the modern world.

At its core, continuous learning is the recognition that knowledge and skills are not static but dynamic and constantly evolving. It is the understanding that what we know today may not be relevant tomorrow, and that we must constantly update our knowledge and skillset to remain competitive and relevant. This requires a shift in mindset from a fixed mindset, where intelligence and abilities are seen as fixed traits, to a growth mindset, where intelligence and abilities are seen as malleable and can be developed through effort and learning.

Continuous learning is not just about acquiring new knowledge; it is also about developing new skills, honing existing ones, and adapting to new ways of thinking and working. It involves a willingness to step outside of one's comfort zone, embrace challenges, and learn from mistakes. It is a lifelong journey of discovery and growth, where the pursuit of knowledge and skills becomes a source of personal and professional fulfillment.

The benefits of continuous learning are numerous and far-reaching. For individuals, continuous learning can lead to increased employability, career advancement, and personal growth. By staying up-to-date with the latest trends and technologies, individuals can make themselves more valuable to employers and open up new career opportunities. Continuous learning can also boost confidence, improve problem-solving skills, and foster a sense of curiosity and lifelong learning.

For organizations, continuous learning can drive innovation, improve performance, and enhance competitiveness. A workforce that is constantly learning and adapting is better equipped to handle challenges, identify opportunities, and develop innovative solutions. Continuous learning can also improve employee engagement and retention, as employees are more likely to feel valued and invested in their work when they are given opportunities to learn and grow.

In the business world, continuous learning is no longer optional. It is a strategic imperative for organizations that want to thrive in today's fast-paced and competitive environment. Companies that invest in continuous learning for their employees are more likely to attract and retain top talent, foster a culture of innovation, and achieve long-term success.

There are many ways to engage in continuous learning. Formal education, such as taking courses or pursuing degrees, is one option. However, continuous learning can also take place through informal channels, such as reading books and articles, attending workshops and conferences, listening to podcasts, or participating in online communities.

The key is to find learning opportunities that are relevant to your interests and goals, and that fit into your schedule and budget. With the rise of online learning platforms and resources, it has never been easier to access high-quality learning materials from anywhere in the world.

Continuous learning is not just about acquiring new knowledge and skills; it is also about applying that knowledge and those skills to real-world problems. This means taking the initiative to seek out opportunities to put your learning into practice, whether it's through volunteering, starting a side project, or taking on new responsibilities at work. By applying what you learn, you can solidify your understanding, gain valuable experience, and make a real impact.

Continuous learning is a lifelong journey, and it is important to celebrate your progress along the way. This can involve setting goals, tracking your progress, and rewarding yourself for your achievements. It can also involve sharing your knowledge and skills with others, mentoring colleagues, or contributing to online communities. By celebrating your learning journey, you can stay motivated and inspired to continue learning and growing.

In conclusion, continuous learning is essential for individuals and organizations alike to thrive in the 21st century. By embracing a growth mindset and investing in ongoing learning and development, we can stay ahead of the curve, adapt to change, and achieve our full potential. Continuous learning is not just a means to an end; it is a rewarding and fulfilling journey that can enrich our lives and empower us to make a positive impact on the world.

ppp

Learning is a lifelong journey. By committing to continuous learning, we can stay ahead of the curve, adapt to new challenges, and achieve our full potential. Remember, the most valuable asset you have is your ability to learn and grow.

TWENTY-THREE
SUMMARY

"The Problem Solver's Toolkit: Creative Solutions for Business Challenges" serves as a comprehensive guide for navigating the complexities and uncertainties of the modern business landscape. It equips readers with a diverse set of tools and strategies to tackle challenges, foster innovation, and achieve sustainable success. Through a multi-faceted approach, the book delves into various aspects of problem-solving, ranging from reframing challenges and harnessing collective creativity to leveraging data-driven insights and embracing continuous learning.

The book commences by emphasizing the importance of reframing challenges. By shifting perspectives and challenging assumptions, businesses can uncover hidden opportunities and unlock innovative solutions. This is exemplified by the story of Kodak, where a failure to reframe the digital revolution led to the company's downfall. The book outlines a step-by-step process for reframing, emphasizing the need to challenge existing mental models and generate new frames to explore alternative solutions.

Brainstorming is another crucial tool in the problem solver's toolkit. The book advocates for brainstorming beyond boundaries, emphasizing the importance of creating a safe and supportive environment where individuals feel comfortable sharing their ideas. It also highlights the significance of divergent and convergent thinking in generating and refining ideas. By incorporating diverse techniques and strategies, such as brainwriting and decision matrices, teams can unleash their collective creativity and arrive at innovative solutions.

Root Cause Analysis (RCA) is presented as a systematic approach to problem-solving that delves deeper than surface-level symptoms. By identifying the underlying causes of problems, organizations can implement effective, long-term solutions that prevent recurrence. The book emphasizes the importance of a thorough investigation, data analysis, and evidence-based decision-making in the RCA process.

Design Thinking is introduced as a human-centric approach to problem-solving. By empathizing with users and understanding their needs, businesses can develop solutions that resonate with their target audience. The book outlines the five stages of Design Thinking: empathize, define, ideate, prototype, and test, emphasizing the iterative nature of the process and the importance of user feedback.

Lean Methodology is explored as a powerful approach to eliminating waste and optimizing processes. By identifying and eliminating non-value-adding activities, organizations can improve efficiency, quality, and customer satisfaction. The book highlights key Lean principles such as pull production and employee empowerment, and it showcases the successful implementation of Lean in various industries.

SWOT analysis is presented as a comprehensive framework for assessing a company's competitive position. By examining internal strengths and weaknesses, as well as external opportunities and threats, businesses can gain a holistic view of their market landscape and develop effective strategies. The book emphasizes the importance of involving diverse stakeholders in the analysis process and regularly updating the SWOT analysis to ensure its relevance.

Scenario planning is introduced as a strategic foresight methodology that helps organizations prepare for potential futures and mitigate risks. By envisioning multiple scenarios, businesses can anticipate the impact of different trends and events, identify potential risks and opportunities, and develop flexible strategies that can adapt to changing circumstances.

The decision matrix is presented as a structured tool for evaluating options objectively and choosing the best path. By systematically assessing alternatives against predetermined criteria, decision-makers can make informed choices that align with their goals. The book emphasizes the importance of choosing relevant criteria, assigning appropriate weights, and basing ratings on objective data.

Mind mapping is explored as a visual tool for capturing, organizing, and visualizing ideas. By creating a graphical representation of information, mind maps can enhance understanding, foster creativity, and improve memory. The book emphasizes the versatility of mind mapping, highlighting its applications in brainstorming, note-taking, planning, problem-solving, and decision-making.

Storytelling is presented as a powerful tool for engaging and inspiring audiences. By crafting compelling narratives that resonate with their target audience, businesses can build brand awareness, foster employee engagement, and drive sales and marketing efforts. The book emphasizes the importance of authenticity, emotional connection, and the use of different mediums in effective storytelling.

Gamification is introduced as a way to transform work into play, boosting motivation and engagement. By incorporating game-design elements and principles into the workplace, organizations can tap into the intrinsic human desire for challenge, achievement, and recognition. The book highlights the benefits of gamification, such as increased motivation, engagement, collaboration, and personalized learning.

Collaboration is emphasized as a key driver of innovation and success. By leveraging collective intelligence, organizations can solve complex problems, generate innovative ideas, and make better decisions. The book discusses the challenges of collaboration, such as overcoming communication barriers and managing conflict, and provides strategies for fostering a collaborative culture.

Experimentation is presented as a fundamental aspect of innovation, with a focus on embracing failure as a learning opportunity. By encouraging a culture of experimentation, organizations can unlock the creative potential of their employees, drive innovation, and achieve long-term success.

Prototyping is explored as a valuable tool for testing and refining ideas before committing to full-scale development. By building quick, iterative models, creators can gather feedback, identify flaws, and improve their designs. The book highlights different types of prototypes, from low-fidelity mockups to high-fidelity interactive prototypes, and emphasizes the importance of choosing the right method for the specific needs of the project.

ppp

Citation And References

This book represents the culmination of extensive research and meticulous analysis, incorporating a diverse range of sources, including numerous books, scholarly studies, and personal experiences. Additionally, I have scoured various websites to gather relevant information and data essential for the compilation of this work. I have taken every precaution to ensure the accuracy of the information presented and have diligently cited all sources to acknowledge their contributions.

Despite these efforts, the possibility of inadvertent errors remains. I deeply value the insights of my readers and appreciate any feedback that can help identify and rectify such inaccuracies. I encourage you to bring any discrepancies to my attention.

Your feedback is not only welcome but crucial, as it will aid in correcting current editions and enhancing the content of future ones. I am committed to maintaining the highest standards of accuracy and reliability in my work and thank you for your support and understanding.

Additionally, I firmly uphold the principle of freedom of speech and expression as guaranteed under Article 19(1)(a) of the Constitution of India, and I respect the diverse viewpoints and expressions of all readers.

ppp

Other Books Of The Author

1. Empowering Minds: A Journey into Women's Self-Discovery and Power
2. The Dynamics of Motivation: Catalyzing Thought into Action
3. Meditation and Mental Well Being: The Path to Inner Peace and Clarity
4. The Psychology of Child Education: Nurturing Future Generations
5. Ethical Enlightenment: A Modern Guide to Living with Integrity
6. Voices of Empowerment: Stories of Women Rising Against Odds
7. Social Psychology in Everyday Life: Understanding Human Connections
8. The Essence of Motivational Speaking: Inspiring Change in Others
9. Balancing Acts: Women, Work, and the Will to Lead
10. Guiding with Grace: Raising Children with Compassion and Awareness
11. The Power of Positive Aging: Embracing Life After Fifty
12. Building Resilient Communities: Social Work in Action
13. The Ethical Educator: Principles for Teaching and Learning
14. From Insight to Impact: Social Psychology for a Better World
15. The Ethics of Empathy: A Guide to Ethical Living
16. The Science of Empowering the Self: Navigating Life's Challenges with Psychological Wisdom
17. The Mindful Conscious Leader: Meditation Techniques for Modern Management
18. Pioneering Spirit: Women's Pathways to Leadership and Empowerment
19. Feeling to Healing: The Role of Emotional Intelligence in Child Development
20. Transformative Talks and Words of Inspiration: Insights into Motivational Oratory

21. Green Ethics: A Path to Sustainable Living
22. Spiritual Integrity: Navigating Life with Moral Compassion
23. Clean Living, Clean Society: The Ethics of Cleanliness
24. Patriotic Spirits: Building a Nation on Positive Attitudes
25. Innovative Integrity & Vibrant Visions: The Ethical and Entrepreneurial Spirit of Gujarat
26. Youthful Visions, Endless Possibilities: Inspiring Ethics and Motivation in Children
27. Living Your Legacy: How to Motivate Others by Living Your Values
28. Secret of Healing Conversations: Ethical Practices in Counselling and Therapy
29. Creative Kindness: Crafting a Life of Compassion and Creativity
30. The Power of Appreciation: How Gratitude Can Transform Your Relationships
31. Bhagavad-Gita: Messages
32. Science of Art: The New Frontier of Fashion Modernism
33. Vivekananda's Virtues: A Blueprint for Modern Living
34. Empower Her: Navigating the Path to Women's Entrepreneurship
35. The Boundless Classroom: Innovations in Global Education
36. The Language of Leadership: Communicating with Authenticity and Impact
37. The Warrior's Mantra: Deciphering the Hanuman Chalisa
38. Echoes of Empathy: Transformative Stories of Social Service
39. Artful Living: Cultivating Creativity in Your Daily Routine
40. Finding Your Why: Discovering Your Passions and Charting Your Course
41. The Role of Social Media in Shaping Self-Esteem and Interpersonal Relationships among Adolescents
42. Karma's Tapestry: Weaving a Life of Selfless Service
43. Altruistic Alchemy: Transforming Lives Through Giving
44. The Blueprint of Pro-Activeness and Productivity: Crafting Habits for Success
45. The Simplicity with Grounded Wisdom: Embracing Authenticity

in a Complex World

46. Secret of Solopreneur's Odyssey: Navigating the Path to Self-Employment

47. Exploring Tapestry of Peace: Global Perspectives on Harmony

48. The Art and Actions of Connection: Mastering Communication for Impact

49. She Governs and at the Helm: Strategies for Political Empowerment

50. Rising Above and Rising with Grace: A Woman's Roadmap to Career Mastery

51. The Effect of Networking & Connectedness: Building Strategic Alliances for Women

52. Beyond his Barriers: Women Thriving in Male-Dominated Fields

53. Secret of Inner Compass: Navigating Life with Intuition

54. Creative & Pro-Active Muses: A Celebration of Women in the Arts

55. Unburdened: The Art of Releasing the Past

56. Amplified Voices: Speeches of Women that Astonished the World

57. Secret of Manifesting Dreams: A Woman's Guide to Intentional Living

58. Ethics and Value Based Education: Reimagining Japan's School System

59. The Moral Compass Curriculum: A Holistic Approach

60. Tech with Heart: Integrating Ethics into Digital Learning

61. Honoring Virtue: Recognizing Ethical Excellence in Education

62. Raising Good Humans: A Guide to Character Development

63. The Spark Within: Nurturing Creativity in Children

64. The Teenager Whisperer: Navigating Adolescence with Grace

65. Igniting a Passion for Learning: Inspiring Lifelong Curiosity

66. The Habit Lab: Cultivating Positive Behaviors in Children

67. Seeds of Empathy: Fostering Compassion in Young Hearts

68. The Reading Revolution: Inspiring a Love of Books in Children

69. The Learning Brain: Unlocking the Secrets of Student Success

70. Teaching for All: Differentiated Instruction Strategies

71. The Time Alchemist: Mastering Time Management for Peak Performance

72. The Resilience Factor: Transforming Setbacks into Stepping Stones

73. The Healing Touch of Nature: An Introduction to Naturopathy

74. Echoes of the Past: Healing Through Past Life Regression

75. The Spiritual Healer's Handbook: Exploring Energy Medicine

76. Crystal Clarity: Unveiling the Power of Gemstones

77. The Dream Weaver's Guide: Decoding the Language of Dreams

78. Emotional Alchemy: Transforming Pain into Power

79. Sonic Serenity: Harnessing Sound for Stress Relief

80. The Entrepreneur's Playbook: Launching Your Business with Confidence

81. Productivity Unleashed: Time Management Strategies for Entrepreneurs

82. The Problem Solver's Toolkit: Creative Solutions for Business Challenges

83. The Future is Now: Emerging Trends in Business

84. The Curious Explorer: A Child's Guide to Scientific Discovery

85. Digital Pioneers: Empowering Kids in the Tech World

86. The Young Philosopher's Guide: Exploring Life's Big Questions

87. Finding Your Voice: Communication Skills for Confident Kids

88. Nature's Playground: A Child's Guide to Outdoor Adventure

89. Growing a Greener Tomorrow: A Guide to Tree Planting & Conservation

90. Driving with Purpose: Ethical Choices on the Road

91. The Healing Touch: Cultivating Compassion in Healthcare

92. Navigating the Digital Landscape: Ethics in the Age of Social Media

93. The Ethical Closet: A Guide to Sustainable Fashion

94. The Mindful Voyager: Sustainable Travel Practices

95. The Feminine Divine: Honoring the Goddesses of India

96. Sacred Sounds: Chanting Your Way to Inner Peace

97. The Yoga Path: Uniting with the Divine Within

98. Rites of Passage: Creating Meaningful Ceremonies

99. The Chakra System: A Map of Inner Transformation

100. Spiritual Sangha: Finding Community through Satsang and

Bhajan

101. Pilgrimage of the Soul: Spiritual Journeys in India

ഉഉഉ

Contact

Dr. Minakshi Bansal
Social Activist
Ahmedabad, Gujarat, Bharat
minakshiindiag20@yahoo.com

ᐅᐅᐅ

|| LOKAHA SAMASTHAHA SUKHINO BHAVANTU ||